The National Map Customer Requirements: Findings from Interviews and Surveys

By Larry Sugarbaker, Kevin E. Coray, and Barbara Poore

Open-File Report 2009–1222

U.S. Department of the Interior
U.S. Geological Survey

U.S. Department of the Interior
KEN SALAZAR, Secretary

U.S. Geological Survey
Suzette M. Kimball, Acting Director

U.S. Geological Survey, Reston, Virginia: 2009

For product and ordering information:
World Wide Web: http://www.usgs.gov/pubprod
Telephone: 1-888-ASK-USGS

For more information on the USGS—the Federal source for science about the Earth, its natural and living resources, natural hazards, and the environment:
World Wide Web: http://www.usgs.gov
Telephone: 1-888-ASK-USGS

Suggested citation:
Sugarbaker, Larry, Coray, K.E., and Poore, Barbara, 2009, *The National Map* customer requirements; Findings from interviews and surveys: U.S. Geological Survey Open-File Report 2009–1222, 34 p. plus appendixes A, B, and C, available only online.

Acknowledgments

This study could not have been completed without the participation of over 2,200 individuals who responded to an invitation for personal interviews or participated in one of the surveys conducted by the Environmental Systems Research Institute (ESRI), the American Society for Photogrammetry and Remote Sensing (ASPRS), or the International Map Trade Association (IMTA). These three organizations initiated surveys so that their constituents could more actively contribute to the assessment of requirements for *The National Map*. They represent a cross section of the geospatial user and mapping community professionals and consumers of the wide range of products and services that make up *The National Map*. The authors wish to thank each and every one of the people who have participated in the study.

The project management team provided guidance throughout the study and directly supported the development of the project plan, the interview questions, and the review of the project progress. They responded with a sense of commitment to fully understand the needs of our customers, and many of the members of the team gave significantly more than the 5 percent of their time that was asked of them. The team members (all of the U.S. Geological Survey) are listed below:

Thomas A. Connolly
John P. Donnelly
Mark A. Eaton
David D. Greenlee
Pat Hytes
Helmut Lestinsky
Vicki Lukas
Elizabeth McCartney
Alan M. Mikuni
Mark R. Newell

Partnership Liaisons were the conduits to our customer base, and they worked to identify hundreds of customers who could contribute to *The National Map* requirements study. They organized and hosted interview sessions across the country and participated in phone interviews when we were unable to travel to a customer site. The authors are indebted to them, and we extend our gratitude and appreciation for this support. Several liaisons spent a significant amount of time serving the needs of the project, and we would especially like to acknowledge these individuals (all of the U.S. Geological Survey):

Sherry L. Durst
Allyson L. Jason
Carol L. Ostergren
Sheri Schneider
Scott D. Van Hoff

Corey Gurnitz, Inc., provided project design and coordination support. Amy McQuade kept the team organized, coordinated 160 plus interviews, and conducted many of the interviews. Her participation in the study was tireless, and we especially want to thank her for helping manage the day-to-day activities of the project.

Contents

Figures

Tables

Conversion Factors

Multiply	By	To obtain
Length		
inch (in.)	2.54	centimeter (cm)
foot (ft)	0.3048	meter (m)

Acronyms

API	application programming interface
ASPRS	American Society for Photogrammetry and Remote Sensing
DEM	digital elevation model
DLG	digital line graph
DLG-3	digital line graph, level 3
ESRI	Environmental Systems Research Institute
FGDC	Federal Geographic Data Committee
GeoPDF	geo-referenced PDF
GIS	geographic information system
GNIS	Geographic Names Information System
GOS	Geospatial One-Stop
IMTA	International Map Trade Association
KML	Keyhole Markup Language
LiDAR	Light Detection And Ranging
NAD 27	North American Datum of 1927
NAD 83	North American Datum of 1983
NED	National Elevation Dataset
NGP	National Geospatial Program
NHD	National Hydrography Dataset
NLCD	National Land Cover Dataset
NPD	National Parcels Dataset
OMB	Office of Management and Budget
PDF	Portable Document Format (Adobe)
PLSS	Public Land Survey System
RSS	Really Simple Syndication or Rich Site Summary
TIFF	tagged image file format
TIGER®	Topologically Integrated Geographic Encoding and Referencing system of the U.S. Census Bureau
TNM	*The National Map*
URL	uniform resource locator
USDA	U.S. Department of Agriculture
USGS	U.S. Geological Survey
UTM/USNG	Universal Transverse Mercator/U.S. National Grid
WBD	Watershed Boundary Dataset
WGS 84	World Geodetic System of 1984

The National Map Customer Requirements: Findings from Interviews and Surveys

By Larry Sugarbaker,[1] Kevin E. Coray,[2] and Barbara Poore[3]

Introduction

The purpose of this study was to receive customer feedback and to understand data and information requirements for *The National Map* (U.S. Geological Survey, 2009). This report provides results and findings from interviews and surveys and will guide policy and operations decisions about data and information requirements leading to the development of a 5-year strategic plan for the National Geospatial Program. These findings are based on feedback from approximately 2,200 customers between February and August 2008. The U.S. Geological Survey (USGS) conducted more than 160 interviews with 200 individuals. The American Society for Photogrammetry and Remote Sensing (ASPRS) and the International Map Trade Association (IMTA) surveyed their memberships and received feedback from over 400 members. The Environmental Systems Research Institute (ESRI) received feedback from over 1,600 of its U.S.-based software users through an online survey sent to customers attending the ESRI International User Conference in the summer of 2008. The results of these surveys were shared with the USGS and have been included in this report.

Background

The National Map (TNM) is a dynamic system of geospatial data and map products and services managed by the U.S. Geological Survey and a network of Federal, State, Tribal, and local partners and other organizations. It is one of the main components of the USGS National Geospatial Program. Geographic information professionals and public map consumers across the country use *The National Map* products and services by the thousands every day. Our customers use maps to enhance their recreational experience and data services to make lifesaving decisions. Nationally consistent geospatial data enable better policy and land management decisions and the effective enforcement of regulatory

responsibilities. However, stakeholder feedback on earlier versions of *The National Map* suggested that the future state of *The National Map* would benefit greatly from a more comprehensive set of customer input. The timing for this input is critical for the USGS as it formulates the 5-year strategic plan for the National Geospatial Program (NGP).

The digital age has fundamentally changed mapping as we understood it 30 years ago. Spatial analysis has moved from a tabletop exercise to fully automated geospatial analysis and scientific modeling. Maps are created today to convey the results of analyses that are performed routinely by consumers of geospatial services. The role of the USGS as the Nation's primary map producer has shifted toward geospatial services. The demand for geographic information system (GIS) products and services is higher than ever, and the demand for traditional paper products has rapidly declined. While there is a need for map products, a number of questions have arisen due to the shift in business paradigms. Who produces maps? What information is displayed on a general-use map? How current do the data need to be? What geospatial data services are needed? What is the appropriate published map scale? Is every map custom made and can the user control the content and self-select the map center? Is the published map always a digital product?

In the emerging Web 2.0 world, the service provision model is shifting. The USGS, while having a long-recognized leadership role in mapping, is taking this opportunity to define its role as a premier geospatial data and application service provider. The shift from maps to geospatial services challenges the notion that a general-purpose base map should be the end result of the service offerings. For this reason, researchers set out to assess customer requirements for the following geospatial data, services, and products:

- Nationally consistent geospatial data

- Quality-assured and integrated geospatial data

- Frequency of update

- Geospatial data delivery services

- Analytical service support through enhanced data models and other features

- Published (digital) map products

[1]U.S. Geological Survey, Reston, VA 20192.

[2]Coray Gurnitz Consulting, Inc., Arlington, VA 22209.

[3]U.S. Geological Survey, St. Petersburg, FL 33701.

The research broadly addressed a full range of business requirements dealing with resource management, hazards assessments, emergency response, outdoor recreation, climate change, national security, environmental regulation, energy, and eight other high-level business functions.

Project Objectives

This customer requirements research project was initiated with three primary objectives:

1. Improve our collective understanding of customer needs for nationally consistent and quality-assured base map data and related geographic information services

2. Receive feedback on topographic map prototype products to support product design and production planning requirements

3. Develop recommendations for improving our marketing, product branding, and customer service operations.

The data-gathering activity identified customer requirements for *The National Map* data and map services (see fig. 1). The data and service needs will directly support the development of *The National Map* 5-year plan. Operational aspects of *The National Map* were not a focus of this study. While customers often wanted to talk about "how" *The National Map* would be built, the study team felt that would be too much of a distraction from the stated purpose of gathering customer requirements. These operational aspects of a functioning national map will be addressed after the requirements are understood and documented.

The USGS has been actively working on new topographic map product development over the last year. Several prototype products have been created, including topographic and orthoimage product maps for 7.5-minute quadrangles. These are digital geo-referenced Adobe Portable Document Format (GeoPDF) files. Several interview and survey questions were developed to guide the topographic mapping activity and to gain initial reaction to the product offerings. The researchers successfully gathered these responses to frame the overall direction. A followup series of focus group meetings to receive detailed responses back from the refined prototypes is planned.

Information Needs Assessment and Data-Collection Activities

Interviews were conducted by USGS representatives from February to May 2008. More than 200 individuals were interviewed across the United States. The interview team

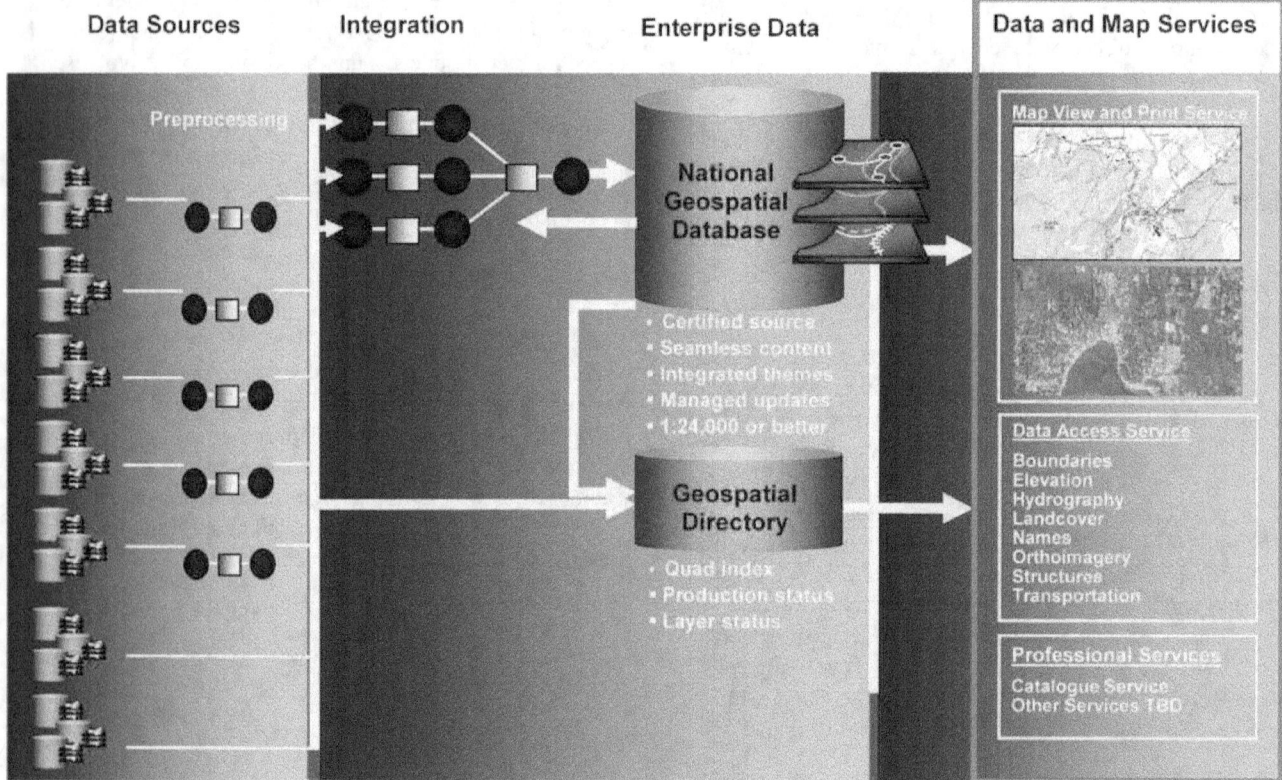

Figure 1. Chart showing product and service outputs for *The National Map* (outlined in red); these outputs were the focus of the customer requirements research project. Business process, partnership development, and roles necessary to define the data workflow within *The National Map* were not a focus of the research activity. Quad, quadrangle; TBD, to be determined.

conducted onsite interviews in Alaska, California, Oregon, Washington, Utah, Colorado, Virginia, Maryland, and Washington, D.C. Phone interviews were used extensively to reach important customers in the Midwest, Southeast, Northeast, and other States where onsite interviews were not possible. Federal agency employees represented 51 percent of the interview pool. State and local government participants made up 30 percent. Other entities such as not-for-profit organizations, commercial GIS service providers, and private sector industry made up the remaining 29 percent. A copy of the structured interview guide can be found in appendix A.

The USGS project management team identified candidate customers to interview. The customers were grouped by organization type and by known business activities within their respective organizations. The objective was to have representative customer groupings across the spectrum of organizations served by the USGS. The customer selection was supported by the USGS network of State and Federal liaisons who possessed firsthand knowledge of existing and potential future customers. USGS liaisons were asked to nominate customers who worked in a variety of settings to include field users of map products, GIS professionals, and managers. USGS liaison regional coordinators compiled these lists and helped prioritize customers for the purpose of selecting individuals across the United States with broad representation of business activities. More than 400 customers were identified through this process. Interviewees were asked to select primary business drivers for their organizations, and these data (see table 1) were used to compile the results tables throughout the report rather than the assigned business drivers used to develop the sample customer list. The project team established a target goal of 175 customers to be interviewed. When the study was completed, 200 individuals had been interviewed in over 160 sessions. Some organizations had two or three individuals participating in the same interview, thus accounting for the higher individual count.

The ASPRS and the IMTA conducted surveys of their memberships in response to the USGS interview request. These surveys were administered by the ASPRS by use of an online survey tool (appendix B) and were nearly identical to the structured interview guide (appendix A). The overall data-gathering activity was greatly enhanced because more than 400 members from these two organizations responded to the requests for input. The distribution of ASPRS and IMTA survey respondents was 35 percent commercial, 18 percent Federal, and 15 percent State and local. The remaining 32 percent of the respondents were distributed across academic, nongovernment organizations, and "other" organizational types. ASPRS and IMTA survey participants self-selected organization type and up to five business drivers for their organization. The distribution of response by organization type and business drivers is therefore assumed to be representative of the organizations' membership. In the tables that follow, the IMTA and ASPRS results are combined. Because the ASPRS administered the survey, the tables are all referenced

as "ASPRS survey," even though results are from both the ASPRS and IMTA memberships.

The Environmental Systems Research Institute (ESRI) developed a short version of the structured interview guide and released a 10-question survey to all ESRI customers residing in the United States and attending the 2008 ESRI International User Conference (appendix C). The online survey invitation was extended to approximately 8,000 individuals. More than 1,600 ArcInfo software users responded to the survey. This was a very significant response rate indicating a high level of interest in the subject matter. The ESRI survey participant distribution was composed of 40 percent State and local government, 19 percent Federal, and 14 percent commercial. The remaining 27 percent were distributed across academic, nongovernment, and "other."

A limitation of the results was that neither the structured interviews nor the surveys conducted by other organizations directly reached consumer groups such as outdoor recreationists. Commercial service providers and Federal managers who work with these groups were interviewed. In addition, while national defense needs were addressed, the response pool was likely small relative to the customer resource commitments in this area. The private sector mineral and forest products industries affecting large portions of the U.S. land base were also not proportionally represented, although Federal program managers working in these areas were interviewed. The graph in figure 2 shows the mix of organization types for the structured interviews, ASPRS survey, and ESRI survey. Even though there were inherent biases in customer representation between the structured interviews and surveys conducted by ASPRS and ESRI, the top-tier base data and service needs were similar between the groups. The project team felt that there was adequate representation across all business and organization types. Consumer product and service needs will be further assessed in focus group sessions designed to gage responses to and interest in specific products such as the topographic map.

Marketing and branding issues were often discussion topics during the interviews. The original interview guide included a question where the interviewee was asked to describe *The National Map*. Generally, customers could not identify many products or services of *The National Map*. Some customers described only *The National Map* viewer. Opinions varied widely about whether or not an older generation printed topographic map was part of *The National Map*. For these reasons, the research team felt that it was better to describe *The National Map* products and service offerings to the customers and to structure the questions around specific products or services. For example, there were no questions like, "Do you use *The National Map* for....?". Instead, a question was structured to rate how often a specific service (like *The National Map* seamless server) was used or how well a customer liked one product compared to a similar offering from another provider. These early findings enabled the research team to refine the interview guide and to significantly improve the data-collection activities. While the

Table 1.   Primary business drivers.

[Primary business drivers as self-identified by interview and survey participants. USGS interview participants could select any number from an established list. Note that table is sorted based on USGS interviews. ASPRS and ESRI survey participants could select their top five business drivers. The "total respondents" is equal to the number of responses received for this particular question and may be less than the total number of surveys or interviews. Source: USGS interview question 2, ASPRS survey question 5.1, ESRI survey question 2]

Primary business activities that use GIS in respondent's organization	USGS interviews		ASPRS survey		ESRI survey		Combined sum	Percent of total
	Yes	Total	Yes	Total	Yes	Total		
Natural resource and land management	70.6%	108	55.7%	210	48.7%	780	1098	51.5%
Natural hazards assessment and emergency response	66.7%	102	32.6%	123	32.4%	519	744	34.9%
Water quantity and quality	54.9%	84	28.1%	106	32.5%	521	711	33.3%
Ecosystems, biodiversity and resource conservation	52.3%	80	35.5%	134	27.0%	433	647	30.3%
Infrastructure development and maintenance	41.8%	64	43.2%	163	51.8%	830	1057	49.6%
Recreation	38.6%	59	10.3%	39	13.7%	219	317	14.9%
Economic development	34.0%	52	23.9%	90	26.4%	423	565	26.5%
Climate change	32.7%	50	20.2%	76	8.0%	128	254	11.9%
Community development and growth management	32.7%	50	34.2%	129	38.6%	619	798	37.4%
Energy and mineral resources	32.0%	49	24.9%	94	16.9%	270	413	19.4%
Human health and the environment	28.8%	44	8.5%	32	12.3%	197	273	12.8%
Law enforcement	27.5%	42	11.1%	42	20.7%	331	415	19.5%
Agricultural practices	26.8%	41	18.3%	69	8.2%	132	242	11.4%
Geography awareness (education)	26.8%	41	20.4%	77	15.6%	250	368	17.3%
Defense and homeland security	22.2%	34	29.7%	112	16.5%	264	410	19.2%
Regulation of pollutants and other contaminants	22.2%	34	8.0%	30	15.7%	252	316	14.8%
Human services	17.0%	26	5.6%	21	9.2%	148	195	9.1%
Total respondents		**153**		**377**		**1602**	**2132**	

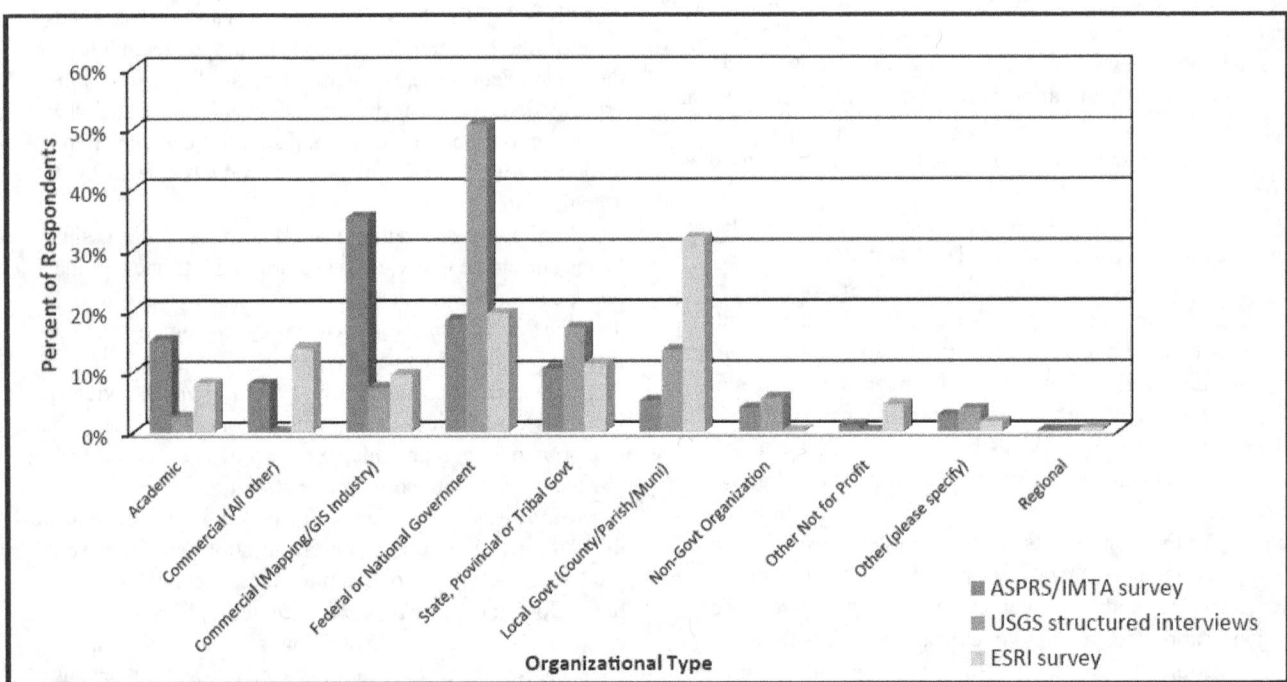

Figure 2.   Organizational type profile of interview and survey participants expressed as a percentage of total participants. The ASPRS-administered survey had 412 association member participants, the USGS structured interviews were conducted with 200 participants (160 interviews), and the ESRI survey was taken by 1,620 GIS professionals.

interview guide went through multiple refinements during the requirements-gathering process, the most substantive changes occurred after the first few interviews conducted in February of 2008.

A series of questions were asked to gain a better understanding of customer knowledge of *The National Map* product offerings. In some instances, customers were asked to compare various Internet services with commercially available services. An important aspect of the one-on-one interviews was to listen to customers and develop a better understanding of their requirements based on what they said about the USGS products and services. Where these needs and insights are not captured in the formal survey responses, the authors have added additional commentary based on their notes and observations captured throughout the interview process.

Results

When customers were asked if they needed access to data beyond their jurisdictional boundaries, 88 percent of respondents said that they did need data from neighboring jurisdictions or nationally to meet their business requirements. When they were asked more specifically how often they needed these data, the distribution of need became clearer. The frequency of need as depicted by local, State, and national level organizations shows that access to these datasets is needed more frequently by organizations with business needs that are national in scope.

Nearly 60 percent of respondents in the structured interviews and in the ASPRS/IMTA surveys said that a topographic map was quite important or very important to meeting their mission needs (table 18). This question was not specifically asked in the ESRI survey, but when asked how important digital or printed USGS topographic quadrangle maps were to their work, 53 percent of ESRI respondents said they were important or very important. Within the ESRI survey, 33 percent of local government respondents said that they were important or very important as compared to 62 percent for all others who responded to the ESRI survey.

Geospatial Base Data Requirements

The National Map is defined by a set of products and services and eight base data layers. The data layers are imagery, elevation, hydrography, geographic names, transportation, land cover, boundaries, and structures. Each of these data layers is composed of more than one data type. For example, boundaries includes county, city, State, and international boundaries, national park boundaries, and many others. These are the data layers that are necessary to support the topographic mapping program of the USGS. In many cases, the USGS relies on partner organizations to provide the data that are ultimately included in *The National Map*. Regardless of the source, an objective of this study was to identify

the most important data layers to be included in *The National Map* and to link those directly with customer-defined business requirements.

Geospatial Data Layer Ranking

Customers were asked to rate the importance of base geospatial datasets relative to their organization's business requirements. This was a forced rating in that customers were required to give seven high, seven medium, and six low ratings. With the exception of parcels and the Public Land Survey System, the 20 geospatial layers identified are subsets of the eight base map data themes currently found in *The National Map*. Customers were asked to rate geospatial base datasets in an effort to gage the national importance of these data relative to other datasets already included in *The National Map*. For this study, the data layers were subdivided into a refined list of 20 base geospatial data layers. While table 2 shows ranking from high to low based on the number of "high" designations from customers in the structured interview, it is important to note that every dataset was ranked high by some customers. The ESRI survey participant ranking of base geospatial datasets is shown in table 3. The ESRI survey presented a slightly different list of base geospatial data layers; thus, the results could not be included in table 2.

Geospatial Data Layer Update Frequency

Customers were asked to identify the minimally acceptable data layer update cycle required to meet their business requirements. Depending on the specific business requirement and the rate of change within any one data layer, the customer needs can be highly variable for even one dataset. Table 4 shows the average response from all customers and represents a general need. It would not be appropriate to interpret the results to mean that a local government official (or any other data steward) could be satisfied with boundary data updated on a 3-year cycle for his or her city or county. However, the majority of regional or national analysis and mapping needs could be satisfied with a 3-year update cycle. Those datasets that have a high rate of change, such as parcels and transportation, would require a very active stewardship and data-integration process. The associated costs of maintaining these datasets must be taken into consideration when designing stewardship models and when completing lifecycle costs analysis.

Customers need access to historical data to support a wide range of business functions. Interview question 12 focused on requirements for consistent and seamless historical spatial data layers to meet a broad set of business needs but did not specifically address the needs to meet legal requirements for records retention. Customers were asked to identify geospatial data layers that were needed to document historical conditions or to meet other requirements. The results depicted in table 5 show that there is a wide distribution of need among

Table 2. Participant ranking of base geospatial datasets from the USGS structured interviews and the ASPRS survey.

[Parcels are not currently part of *The National Map* base data themes. *N,* number of participant responses. Source: USGS interview question 9, ASPRS survey question 9.1–9.2]

Ranking of base geospatial data layers	Structured interviews				ASPRS survey			
	N	Low	Med	High	N	Low	Med	High
Orthoimagery	158	3%	10%	87%	276	9%	11%	80%
Transportation - Public streets/roads	158	7%	17%	76%	271	7%	21%	72%
Elevation	158	7%	20%	73%	275	4%	15%	82%
Hydrography – Surface water	158	8%	23%	70%	268	11%	30%	59%
Boundaries – Civil boundaries e.g. city, county, state	158	14%	31%	55%	266	16%	37%	47%
Parcels	158	24%	28%	48%	268	35%	30%	35%
Boundaries - Public Land Survey System	158	29%	33%	39%	268	28%	33%	40%
Land cover (e.g. vegetation, built, wetlands)	156	23%	41%	36%	267	16%	34%	50%
Geographic names	158	21%	46%	33%	268	24%	43%	33%
Vertical and horizontal control	158	23%	45%	32%	268	19%	25%	56%
Boundaries – Federal and Native American lands	157	23%	47%	30%	261	37%	36%	27%
Structures – selected public buildings such as schools	158	39%	34%	27%	265	26%	45%	29%
Pipelines and powerlines	158	22%	53%	25%	268	37%	36%	27%
Transportation – Other routes e.g. forest roads	155	37%	45%	19%	265	41%	41%	19%
Transportation – Airports	157	42%	42%	16%	263	38%	38%	24%
Springs and wells	157	46%	38%	16%	268	53%	32%	16%
Transportation – Railroads	158	39%	46%	16%	265	31%	44%	25%
Structures – rural areas	158	48%	37%	15%	261	39%	42%	19%
Physiographic feature names (e.g. mountain, valley.)	158	41%	44%	15%	269	43%	33%	24%
Transportation – Trails	157	41%	46%	13%	264	50%	36%	14%

Table 3. Participant ranking of base geospatial datasets from the ESRI survey.

[The ESRI survey presented a slightly different list of base geospatial data layers due in part to the omission of three data layers. In addition, the parcels layer was split into public and private to determine if there would be a significant difference in ranking or requirements for this geospatial data layer. For these reasons, a side-by-side comparison with data from the USGS interviews and the ASPRS survey was not possible. *N,* number of participant responses. Source: ESRI survey question 4]

Ranking of base geospatial data layers	ESRI survey - all respondents			ESRI survey - local government only			ESRI survey - TOTAL without local government		
5 - very important, 4 - quite important, 3 - somewhat important, 2 - not very important, 1 - do not use (Percent favorable = very - somewhat important)	Average	Percent favorable	Total	Average	Percent favorable	Total	Average	Percent favorable	Total
Transportation— Public streets and roads	4.39	85%	1581	4 39	86%	500	4.38	85%	1081
Boundaries— Civil boundaries (city, county, state, international)	4.28	83%	1588	4.15	80%	500	4.35	85%	1088
Orthoimagery	4.25	79%	1571	4 23	79%	492	4.27	79%	1079
Elevation	4.13	78%	1580	3 96	74%	494	4.22	80%	1086
Hydrography— Surface water	4.07	76%	1583	3 85	70%	496	4.18	79%	1087
Utilities (regional and interstate pipelines and power lines)	3.95	71%	1577	4 04	76%	495	3.91	69%	1082
Land cover (e.g. vegetation, built, wetlands, and grasslands)	3.93	70%	1580	3 67	62%	494	4.05	74%	1086
Boundaries— PLSS (section, township, range)	3.89	68%	1576	3.75	64%	496	3.96	70%	1080
Transportation— Railroads	3.77	64%	1579	3.71	63%	496	3.80	65%	1083
Structures— Selected public buildings (e.g. schools, hospitals)	3.74	62%	1575	3 94	73%	497	3.65	57%	1078
Hydrography— Springs and wells	3.69	61%	1556	3 56	58%	490	3.75	63%	1066
Transportation— Airports	3.67	58%	1576	3 62	59%	495	3.69	58%	1081
Boundaries— Federal and Native American lands	3.57	57%	1569	3.02	39%	490	3.82	65%	1079
Physiographic feature names (e.g. mountain, valley)	3.52	53%	1562	3.28	44%	488	3.63	57%	1074
Transportation— Trails	3.51	52%	1568	3.53	55%	493	3.50	51%	1075
Structures— Buildings in rural areas	3.50	52%	1574	3 50	55%	495	3.50	51%	1079

Table 4.   Average minimally acceptable update cycles to meet business requirements for base data themes.

[Source: USGS interview question 11]

Base geospatial data layer	Update cycle
Parcels	≤ 1 year
Transportation - Public streets/roads	≤ 1 year
Boundaries – Civil boundaries to include city, county, state, international	≤ 3 years
Orthoimagery	≤ 3 years
Geographic names	≤ 3 years
Boundaries – Federal and Native American lands	≤ 3 years
Hydrography – Surface water	≤ 3 years
Boundaries - Public Land Survey System	≤ 3 years
Structures – selected public buildings such as schools, hospitals, courthouse	≤ 3 years
Pipelines and powerlines	≤ 3 years
Vertical and horizontal control	≤ 3 years
Land cover (i.e. vegetation, built, wetlands, grasslands)	≤ 3 years
Structures – rural areas	≤ 3 years
Transportation – Trails	≤ 3 years
Transportation – Airports	≤ 3 years
Springs and wells	≤ 3 years
Transportation – Other routes such as forest roads generally closed to public	≤ 3 years
Transportation – Railroads	≤ 3 years
Physiographic feature names (mountain, valley, canyon, plain, etc.)	≤ 5 years
Elevation	≤ 5 years

Table 5.   Geospatial data layer historical or archival needs.

[Side-by-side comparison of results from the USGS structured interviews and the ASPRS survey for base geospatial data layers that are needed to meet archival or historical data access requirements. Source: USGS interview question 12, ASPRS survey question 11.2]

Base geospatial data layer	Structured interview		ASPRS survey	
	Yes	Total	Yes	Total
Orthoimagery	75.7%	103	88.5%	215
Land cover (i.e. vegetation, built, wetlands, grasslands)	51.5%	70	56.4%	137
Parcels	39.7%	54	39.9%	97
Boundaries – Civil boundaries to include city, county, state, international	32.4%	44	35.8%	87
Hydrography – Surface water	30.1%	41	38.3%	93
Transportation - Public streets/roads	27.2%	37	40.3%	98
Geographic names	22.8%	31	31.7%	77
Boundaries – Federal and Native American lands	19.9%	27	17.3%	42
Structures – rural areas	16.9%	23	20.2%	49
Boundaries - Public Land Survey System	16.9%	23	22.2%	54
Elevation	15.4%	21	29.6%	72
Structures – selected public buildings such as schools, hospitals, courthouse	14.7%	20	18.9%	46
Springs and wells	14.0%	19	15.2%	37
Transportation – Railroads	11.8%	16	22.6%	55
Vertical and horizontal control	11.0%	15	33.3%	81
Transportation – Trails	10.3%	14	15.6%	38
Transportation – Other routes such as forest roads generally closed to public	9.6%	13	12.8%	31
Pipelines and powerlines	9.6%	13	21.4%	52
Physiographic feature names (mountain, valley, canyon, plain, etc.)	9.6%	13	15.2%	37
Transportation – Airports	5.9%	8	13.2%	32
Total number of respondents to this question		136		243

data layers but that maintaining a few historical data layers, such as orthoimagery and land cover, could meet a majority of the need. The interview team did not formally capture the business activities for historical data; however, the need for geospatial data to support analysis of land cover and environmental change was mentioned by many customers during informal discussions.

Geospatial Data Layer Scale and Resolution

Interview and survey respondents were asked to rate their needs for scale and resolution of different data layers. Results shown in table 6 were grouped by local, State, regional, or national responsibilities based on the customer's organization type. As might be expected, local organizations rated fine-resolution data more highly while national organizations said they needed data at a mid scale of 1:24,000 more frequently. However, organizations at each level expressed a need for data at all scales. While this study did not attempt to assess requirements by region or State, it is likely that a more refined assessment by location would yield a better set of requirements. Any national program, therefore, should consider the geographic distribution of need based on primary business drivers. It was not within the scope of this project to determine detailed requirements by location and it is unlikely that the sample size would yield significant new insight into the requirements if attempts were made to further isolate the analysis to specific geographic regions of the country. To further refine the results would require sampling customer requirements by local, regional, and national levels for a number of business applications. It is important to recognize that local does not always mean urban. Local needs can range from urban tax assessment to agriculture operations and forest management. Likewise,

there may be important national level needs to evaluate urban conditions. While not statistically significant, an important observation made during the study was that resource management operations are trending toward 1:12,000-scale data and higher resolution elevation and imagery data acquisition programs.

The discussion of geospatial data scale and resolution was often influenced by concerns for computing capacity and network bandwidth needed to utilize very large datasets. Customers found it difficult to think about the business problems they were trying to address apart from these technical limitations that affected work productivity. Conversely, it is important that the USGS not build national datasets at a scale or resolution that is affordable if they do not meet the customer requirements. This is a significant consideration as the USGS continues to plan for the future, knowing that technology will continue to improve and that costs to acquire high-resolution data should decline with improved technology.

Orthoimagery

Orthoimagery consistently was cited one of the top datasets needed to support geospatial activities regardless of the business activity or application level. Although a 1-meter national dataset meets a large number of needs, there is also a call for 12-inch-resolution data. At 12-inch resolution, a significant number of local needs are also addressed. A 3-year update cycle is the minimally acceptable update frequency. Accessibility of historical imagery was identified as the number one data archive need. While the USGS is actively archiving historical imagery, there is a need to determine if there is a role for *The National Map* to address some of this need in the context of the vision to provide access to seamless geospatial base data.

Table 6.   Resolution and scale requirements grouped by local, State, regional, and national.

[The expressed needs are distributed across all scales and resolutions. The numeric responses were based on a five-point rating scale, where 5 is very important, 4 is quite important, 3 is somewhat important, 2 is not very important, and 1 indicates that a customer has no need for this resolution or scale data. *N*, number of participant responses; Std. Dev., standard deviation. Source: USGS interview question 13]

Resolution and scale requirements		Imagery				Elevation				Lines and areas (vector data)			
		6 inch	12 inch	1 meter	2 5 meter	sub-meter	3 meter	10 meter	30 meter	1:12,000+	1 24,000	1:63,360	1:100,000
Local	Mean	4.11	4.07	3 00	2.19	3.71	3.02	2.77	2.18	3.95	3.14	1.98	1.84
	N	22	22	22	21	21	22	22	22	22	22	22	22
	Std. Dev.	1.15	1.05	1 20	1.33	1 31	1.30	1.51	1.33	1.46	1.39	1.22	1.06
State	Mean	3 00	3.42	4 06	2.30	3 32	3.27	3.33	2.67	3.79	3.96	2.40	2.42
	N	48	48	48	37	37	48	48	48	48	48	48	48
	Std. Dev.	1.20	1.33	1 08	1.27	1.40	1.38	1.42	1.46	1.29	1.30	1.30	1.37
Regional	Mean	2.67	3.00	4 00	3.23	3 55	3.23	3 63	3.08	4.09	4.54	3.13	3.50
	N	24	24	24	22	22	24	24	24	22	24	24	24
	Std. Dev.	1.13	1.22	1.18	1.23	1.47	1.16	1 31	1.41	0.87	0.59	1.08	0.98
National	Mean	2.89	3.41	3.98	3.19	3.08	3.63	3.96	3.37	3.81	4.02	3.28	3 04
	N	54	54	54	52	53	54	53	52	52	53	53	53
	Std. Dev.	1 31	1.39	1 22	1.31	1.34	1.17	1.24	1.34	1.03	1.07	1.38	1.34
Total	Mean	3 07	3.44	3 86	2.79	3 32	3.36	3.52	2.91	3.87	3.95	2.77	2.73
	N	148	148	148	132	133	148	147	146	144	147	147	147
	Std. Dev.	1 29	1.32	1 21	1.36	1 38	1.27	1.40	1.44	1.17	1.20	1.37	1.36

Transportation

The transportation dataset was identified as one of the most important geospatial datasets. However, subcomponents of the transportation data layer that include airports, trails, forest roads closed to the general public, and railroads are in the lower one-third of the overall priority ranking of base geospatial datasets. Transportation data pose one of the most demanding stewardship challenges, given the need for current data and the complex array of uses. In addition, there are limited resources available at the USGS to support maintenance of transportation data, and customers often asked how the Department of Transportation was fulfilling its data steward-ship responsibilities required by OMB Circular A–16 (Office of Management and Budget, 2002).

A wide range of options were suggested by customers for meeting the need for transportation data. Although high-quality commercial datasets are available for public streets and highways, customers expressed the need to have unrestricted access to the data. Unrestricted access to some commercial datasets should not be ruled out as a solution because there may be a willingness on the part of commercial transportation data providers to make a subset of their data available through an unrestricted public use license. Other ideas identified by customers included utilizing the updated TIGER® data (U.S. Census Bureau, 2009) and implementing an active steward-ship program with States in an effort to build a sustainable and managed transportation dataset for the Nation. Another commonly suggested solution would be to initiate a pilot project to test a wiki-based approach to developing an open-source transportation dataset.

Elevation

Quality improvements to elevation data were often cited as a high-priority need. Much of the National Elevation Data-set is composed of scanned topographic map contours that were converted to 10-meter digital elevation models (DEMs). Over time, hydrography and other datasets have been modified and no longer align with the elevation. There has also been a growing need for very accurate elevation data to support resource and land use planning, flood mapping activities, particularly in coastal areas, and detailed geological mapping. The growing need for a refined national elevation dataset calls for stepped up attention in this area. Light Detection And Ranging (LiDAR) was often referred to as the logical tech-nology solution to address this need. The business case for a national LiDAR program is significantly strengthened when one considers the opportunity to improve multiple data layers in *The National Map,* such as refined definition of surface water features, land cover (primarily tree canopy), elevation models having resolutions of less than 1 meter, and improved identification of infrastructure.

Hydrography

The National Hydrography Dataset (NHD) was recently completed for 1:24,000-scale coverage over the conterminous United States. This was hailed as a major accomplishment by customers, and the Web services are used more often by interviewed customers than either Geospa-tial One-Stop or *The National Map* viewer. The NHD has a faithful following, and there is a growing list of value-added services that use the NHD. The NHD is also being transitioned to a stewardship maintenance program whereby States are actively taking on data maintenance responsibilities. In spite of these accomplishments, the NHD was one of the datasets most often cited as needing better quality control, and the level of integration with the National Elevation Dataset (NED) was not sufficient to meet analysis or basic mapping needs. When customers were asked about the need for other datasets in *The National Map,* watershed boundaries received one of the high-est ratings. The NHD will soon include the Watershed Bound-ary Dataset (WBD), which is under development by a con-sortium of agencies. Springs and wells, which are part of the hydrography theme definition for hydrography, were ranked 13th in importance out of 20 surveyed data layers.

Boundaries

To better understand the boundaries requirement, custom-ers were asked to rank their need for civil boundaries as well as boundaries of Federal and Tribal lands. In the part of the survey and interview that included questions on map products (see fig. 3), the example was shown where a county boundary was represented in two different places. Customers expressed the lowest levels of tolerance for this type of error. Civil boundaries include boundaries of local to international signifi-cance, yet they are all included in one geospatial data layer. Consequently, it has been difficult to identify a single reliable source for these data.

Parcels

The National Research Council, Committee on Land Parcel Databases (2007), concluded that complete national land parcel data are necessary, timely, technically feasible, and affordable. The committee described the need for a wide range of parcel and parcel-related data and made recommendations for stewardship responsibilities covering Federal, Tribal, and all other publicly and privately owned parcels. In consider-ation of these findings, a general category for parcel data was added to the data layer prioritization questions for geospatial base data layers, even though parcels are not part of *The National Map* today. Parcels ranked number 6 out of 20 data layers (table 2). Parcel data needs were split into public and private lands in the ESRI survey and included in the "other" geospatial data layers question. When compared in this way to other geospatial data layers that may be considered for inclusion in *The National Map*, both public and private parcels made up two of the top four geospatial data layers. The ESRI survey data for "other geospatial data layers" were further analyzed to determine what effect local government needs for parcel data had on the overall priority. While the local government requirements for parcels were slightly higher, the overall importance rating changed very little. Both private and public parcel data fell within the top five data layers even when local requirements were not considered. Table 9, discussed below in this report, shows the results of this analysis and the ranking of other geospatial data layers.

The development of a National Parcels Dataset (NPD) poses important challenges that must be addressed. For most applications, customers require data that are current within 1 year, the source datasets are distributed across cities and counties, and restrictions on access by some local governments must be overcome. Regardless of these difficulties, the need is real, and the work to create a national dataset should be pursued.

Public Land Survey System

The need for Public Land Survey System (PLSS) data fell in the middle of the prioritized list (table 2). The strong requirement for Western States to have access to accurate public land survey data is not evident in this ranking, even though customers in the West expressed this as a high-level need. The interviews (and ASPRS survey) could not be parsed by geography, but it was clear in the interviews that the requirement in the Western States was much higher than in the "metes and bounds" States of the East. The Bureau of Land Management oversees the development and support of the national PLSS dataset. Historically, the PLSS was displayed on the USGS topographic maps of 7.5-minute quadrangles. When *The National Map* plan was created in 2001, the PLSS was not included in the eight base data themes composing the national geospatial database. The survey results indicate that this decision should be revisited.

Land Cover

Land cover requirements are being met by analysis of Landsat data to create seamless coverage of classified land categories equivalent to the level 2 Anderson classification system; the update cycle is moving from 10 to 5 years. Currently, there are completed analyses for 1992 and 2001. The Landsat image base is 30-meter data and has the lowest level of resolution of any dataset in *The National Map*. Land cover was ranked number 8 out of 20 base geospatial data layers. However, when customers were asked about importance from a historical perspective, it received the second highest ranking among 20 datasets. In essence, land cover data become more valuable over time to understand long-term change and to support analysis of climate change and other important scientific and socioeconomic trends. The acceptable update cycle of 3

years suggests the need to move to a more frequent update cycle than the planned 5-year cycle.

Geographic Names

The Geographic Names Information System (GNIS) was developed by the USGS in cooperation with the U.S. Board on Geographic Names. It contains information about the proper names for places, features, and areas in the 50 States, the District of Columbia, and the territories and outlying areas of the United States. There are about 2 million geographic names in the system, which also supports the production of maps in the USGS. Customers often recognized the importance of the Geographic Names Information System as a source of high-quality information about named features. Names ranked relatively high (upper half) on the list of priority data layers (table 2).

Structures

The requirements for data on structures (buildings) within *The National Map* have been the focus of much discussion. Overall, customers placed their need for structures data in the bottom half when compared to other requirements (see table 2). Customers ranked public buildings and other critical infrastructure such as hospitals and schools (structures in urban areas) higher than structures generally found in rural areas. Customers from organizations who listed as primary business drivers homeland security, human services, or emergency response had a higher need for structures in urban areas than did other customers (significant positive correlations shown in table 7). Further, table 7 shows that needs for structures in urban areas were ranked lower by customers with ecosystems, recreation, water quality, natural resource management, climate change, and geography awareness as primary business drivers (significant negative correlations). No significant correlations were found between business drivers and rural structures.

While breadth of need may not be the sole basis for determining whether or not a dataset should be included in *The National Map*, it is a reasonable criterion to use in determining authoritative source communities and probable sources of funding. As such, since structures in general and structures in rural areas in particular received some of the lowest rankings of all the base data layers, it could be asked what Federal entity should have the responsibility for maintaining a national dataset.

Other Geospatial Data Requirements

USGS interview and ASPRS survey participants were asked to rate the importance of geospatial selected data layers that are not currently included within *The National Map*. As shown in table 8, all 12 data layers were ranked as "somewhat

Table 7. Structures data needs by business drivers.

[Business drivers correlated with importance ranking for structures in urban areas, listed from highest magnitude positive correlation (that is, higher importance ranking of urban structures) to highest magnitude negative correlations (that is, lower importance ranking of urban structures). Customers with business drivers of defense and homeland security (r = .27), human services, or natural hazards assessment and emergency response tended to rank need for urban structures higher than customers with other business drivers. Conversely, those with drivers of ecosystems, biodiversity, and resource conservation tended to rank urban structures lower in importance (r = -.36). Customers with business drivers with insignificant correlations (significance greater than .05) suggest no tendency for urban structures to be ranked higher, lower, or average. N, number of participant responses. Source: USGS interview question 9, structures, correlated with question 2, business drivers]

Primary business activities	Pearson correlation	Significance (2-tailed)	N
Defense and homeland security	0.272	0.001	149
Human services	0.215	0.008	149
Natural hazards assessment and emergency response	0.170	0.038	149
Infrastructure development and maintenance	0.099	0.229	149
Community development and growth management	0.058	0.483	149
Regulation of pollutants and other contaminants	0.053	0.523	149
Human health and the environment	0.030	0.718	149
Law enforcement	0.009	0.909	149
Economic development	-0.042	0.608	149
Agricultural practices	-0.123	0.134	149
Energy and mineral resources	-0.155	0.059	149
Geography awareness (education)	-0.164	0.046	149
Climate change	-0.176	0.032	149
Natural resource and land management	-0.196	0.016	149
Water quantity and quality	-0.203	0.013	149
Recreation	-0.216	0.008	149
Ecosystems, biodiversity and resource conservation	-0.361	0.000	149

Table 8. Other geospatial data requirements from the USGS structured interviews and the ASPRS survey.

[Interview and survey participants were given an opportunity to rate data layers that may be needed but that are not currently in *The National Map*. The ratings were recorded on a five-point scale, where 5 equals very important and 1 indicates the data layer is not needed or used by the participant's organization. It is noted that the data from the cooperative project to create and update the watershed boundaries is being incorporated into the National Hydrography Dataset (NHD) and is now part of *The National Map*. N, number of participant responses. Source: USGS interview question 14, ASPRS survey question 12.2]

Other geospatial data layer 5 - very important, 4 - quite important, 3 - somewhat important, 2 - not very important, 1 - do not use	Structured interviews		ASPRS survey		Weighted average
	Mean	N	Mean	N	
Land use	4.14	144	3.78	232	3.92
Hydrography-watershed boundaries	4.08	151	3.60	228	3.79
Wetlands	3.90	153	3.63	231	3.74
Flood zones	3.85	127	3.43	228	3.58
Soils	3.58	153	3.34	229	3.44
Ground water	3.53	153	3.04	227	3.24
Ecological Units or Systems (bog, wetland etc.)	3.47	152	3.25	222	3.34
Utilities	3.42	153	3.33	227	3.37
Geology	3.38	153	3.07	227	3.19
Biodiversity (species and ecosystems at risk)	3.24	152	2.97	223	3.08
Zoning	3.14	150	2.90	223	3.00
Bathymetry	2.90	153	2.81	228	2.85

important" or higher, indicating a high interest for additional national data layers.

The ESRI survey was issued after the USGS interviews and the ASPRS survey were completed. There was considerable community interest that emerged for LiDAR data and for a national parcel dataset. The earlier USGS interviews asked customers to rank parcels against base data layers and didn't specifically assess LiDAR. The interview team addressed the question about LiDAR by asking more detailed questions about elevation needs. Throughout the interviews, customers consistently pointed out the other values of LiDAR and wanted to know why they were not asked to rate that as a dataset (as opposed to a technology). In addition to the inclusion of LiDAR, the ESRI survey also split parcels into publicly and privately held lands to see if one parcel type were needed more than the other. Local government users were the largest user group represented in this survey, and their results are also shown separately for comparison purposes in table 9.

Among other geospatial data layers, flood zones, parcels (both publicly owned and privately owned), LiDAR, and land use all had percent favorable ratings greater than 75 percent. Except for LiDAR (76 percent favorable for local government, 78 percent favorable for others), local government rated these items even higher in importance (81 percent or greater favorable). Also note that the ESRI total sample shows a less than 50 percent favorable importance rating for ecological systems, biodiversity, and bathymetry. An analysis of local government users compared to all other user groups indicates that local government had a lower need for these data layers and that their responses had the overall effect of lowering the importance ratings.

Data Quality and Quality Control

A series of general data and map quality questions were asked in order to understand customer sensitivity to quality as it relates to geospatial features and how current, accurate, and complete they are in a database (see table 10). In some cases, questions were posed in such a way as to force customers to select an answer that required them to make a tradeoff decision. This was done in part to help the USGS prioritize data improvement objectives while recognizing that obtaining high-quality data is a goal for everyone.

Many of the data that come to the USGS are acquired by partner Federal and State agencies. When data flow into the national database from multiple sources, the need for a unified data quality and integration program becomes apparent. Customers were asked to rate how important it is for the USGS to implement a quality-control program for selected data layers. Although there was not a large rating difference, the transportation data were rated more highly than others.

Table 9. Other geospatial data requirements from the ESRI survey.

[The ESRI survey included additional datasets in the "other geospatial data layer" question and is therefore presented separately. The average score is computed from a five-point scale, where 5 is very important and 1 is not important. Percent favorable is determining the percent of "important" and "very important" responses selected by the survey participant. Source: ESRI survey question 5]

Other geospatial data layer 5 - very important, 4 - important, 3 - somewhat important, 2 - less than important, 1 - not important	ESRI survey - All respondents			ESRI survey - Local government only			ESRI Survey - TOTAL without local government		
	Average	Percent favorable	Total	Average	Percent favorable	Total	Average	Percent favorable	Total
Flood zones	4.24	81%	1583	4.35	86%	499	4.19	79%	1084
Parcels— Publicly owned	4.22	79%	1578	4.32	83%	501	4.17	78%	1077
LiDAR - for detailed topography and other mapping activities	4.17	77%	1575	4.11	76%	494	4.20	78%	1081
Parcels— Privately owned	4.16	77%	1577	4.30	81%	501	4.10	75%	1076
Land use	4.15	79%	1571	4.17	81%	493	4.14	78%	1078
Utilities (local water, sewer, electrical, and natural gas)	4.02	73%	1570	4.22	81%	496	3.93	69%	1074
Vertical and horizontal control	3.82	64%	1557	3.95	68%	490	3.77	62%	1067
Ground water	3.82	66%	1563	3.80	67%	491	3.83	66%	1072
Soils	3.76	64%	1568	3.63	60%	497	3.83	66%	1071
Transportation— Other routes such as forest roads	3.76	62%	1567	3.67	60%	492	3.80	63%	1075
Geology	3.75	64%	1567	3.53	55%	491	3.85	67%	1076
Zoning	3.62	55%	1575	3.98	70%	499	3.46	48%	1076
Ecological systems (e.g., oak woodland, swale grassland)	3.43	50%	1555	3.02	36%	484	3.61	56%	1071
Biodiversity (species and ecosystems at risk)	3.33	47%	1556	2.88	33%	484	3.53	54%	1072
Bathymetry	3.13	40%	1545	2.61	25%	476	3.35	48%	1069

Table 10. Importance of data quality control program for selected base geospatial data layers coming from multiple sources.

[*N*, number of participant responses. Source: USGS interview question 27, ASPRS survey question 16.2]

Importance of a quality control program 1 - not very important, 3 - somewhat important, 5 - critically important	Structured interview		ASPRS survey	
	N	Mean	*N*	Mean
Quality program for roads	129	4.37	211	4.21
Quality program for hydrography (water features)	130	4.31	210	4.08
Quality program for boundaries	129	4.11	214	4.07
Quality program for contours	129	4.09	212	4.02
Quality program for names of features	129	3.92	213	3.61

Positional (coordinates describing the geographic location) accuracy (see table 11) was identified as the most important quality-control issue over attribute accuracy, completeness, and currency. This particular question received a great deal of discussion during the structured interviews. Many customers did not want to be put in a position of ranking one data quality component over another, indicating that they are all critically important. There was a view, however, that positional accuracy of features was a core component of a quality database and that a maintenance program would more effectively address improvements in the form of new features or correction of attributes. It would be difficult to improve overall positional accuracy unless it were accomplished through a complete data recompilation.

Geospatial integration of data coming from multiple sources has long been recognized as a significant issue. While integration is considered to be a component of data quality, it is also recognized that customers have different sensitivities for integration issues related to different data subjects. When customers were presented with map images of known data errors, they were most sensitive to errors in boundary representations (table 12). The example they were shown was of a county boundary from two different sources (fig. 3). Also, four examples of elevation contour and hydrography conflicts were presented. It was viewed as a more significant problem when hydrography and elevation contours did not match (fig.

4A, 4B). Customers were not as concerned about hydrographic features that did not match current watercourses within defined stream channels (fig. 4C). Contours that did not match a transportation cut-and-fill feature were found to be more acceptable (fig. 5A). Customers were more tolerant of cartographic over posting of feature names or shorelines that didn't fully match an orthoimage (fig. 5B, 5C).

Customer Requirements—Online Functionality

The USGS provides a broad range of online geospatial services to meet customer requirements. These services range from specific data community services for the NHD to access to wide-ranging partner datasets through *The National Map* viewer and Geospatial One-Stop (GOS). Some of the services provide similar functionality, and they range in age from a few years old to current releases. A series of questions were designed to elicit some very basic answers about customer experience with various online services and their need for improved services. The questions were intended to get feedback more specifically on *The National Map* service needs.

A number of questions were asked generally about the types of services needed. Additional questions were more focused on actual USGS mapping services. Regardless of how the questions were asked or what specific service was being evaluated, customers almost always valued services that gave

Table 11. Assessment of customer priorities for quality control.

[Positional accuracy ranked significantly higher than other quality components. *N*, number of participant responses. Source: USGS interview question 36, ASPRS survey question 17.4]

| Customer priorities for quality control | Structured interviews | | ASPRS survey | |
1 - highest importance to 4 - lowest importance	*N*	Average Rank	*N*	Average Rank
Positional accuracy of features	115	1.76	198	1.50
Currency (recent date) of features	115	2.63	201	2.68
Completeness of features	115	2.67	198	2.96
Attribute accuracy of features	116	2.79	195	2.76

Table 12. Customer sensitivity to errors on topographic maps.

[Customers were asked to rate acceptability of known errors on maps relative to their business requirements. A lower mean response indicates that a customer is more sensitive to errors. Note that the ASPRS survey assigned a 1 to fully acceptable and a 3 to not acceptable. For comparison purposes, the values are reversed in this table. *N*, number of participant responses. Source: USGS interview question 39, ASPRS survey question 18.1–21.1]

| Sensitivity to feature conflicts found on sample maps | Structured interviews | | ASPRS survey | |
1 - not acceptable, 2 - can live with it, 3 - fully acceptable	*N*	Mean	*N*	Mean
Shoreline vector does not align with ortho image shoreline	129	2.02	186	2.55
Offset issues and over posting issues	129	1.78	181	2.35
Misalignments and un-updated contours	130	1.75	168	2.26
Hydrography vector does not match the newer ortho image	129	1.71	172	2.56
Hydrography that does not follow contour lines	129	1.53	181	2.44
Contour lines crossing water features	128	1.52	154	2.26
Boundaries shown differently from different data sources	128	1.45	170	1.92

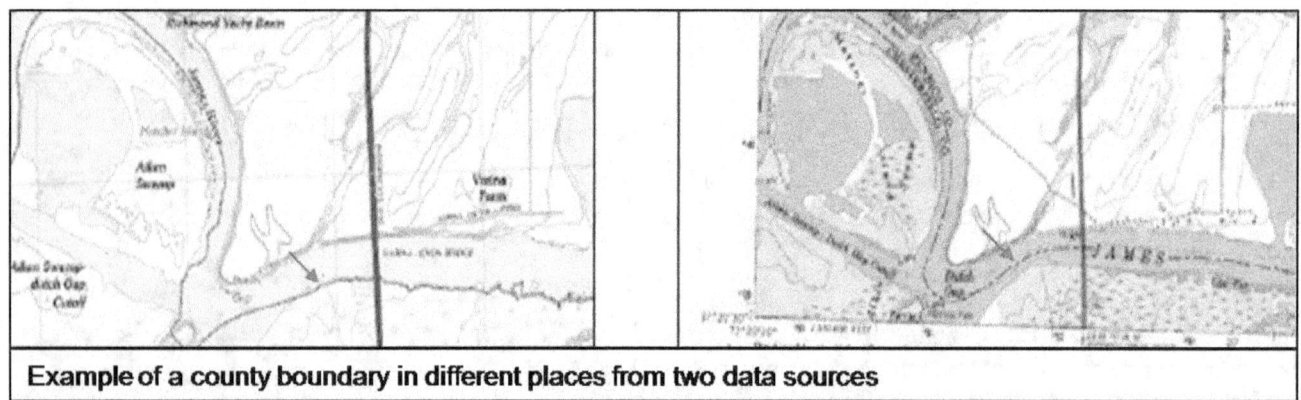

Example of a county boundary in different places from two data sources

Figure 3.   Maps depicting a county boundary in two locations from different sources. Customers expressed the lowest level of acceptance for boundary errors when presented with a number of scenarios.

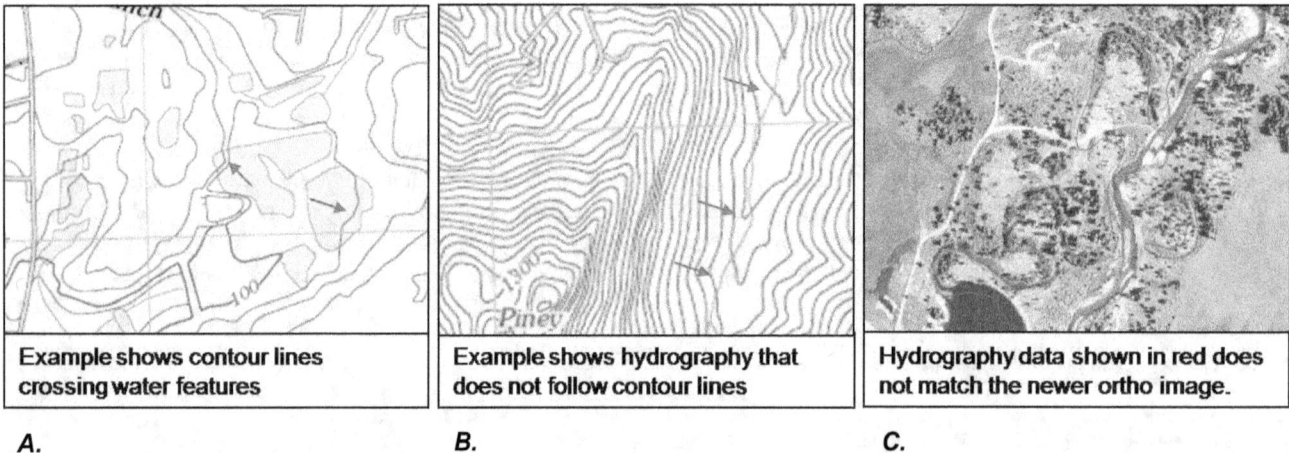

| Example shows contour lines crossing water features | Example shows hydrography that does not follow contour lines | Hydrography data shown in red does not match the newer ortho image. |

A.   *B.*   *C.*

Figure 4.   Maps and orthoimage showing (*A*) contour lines crossing water features, (*B*) hydrography not following contour lines, and (*C*) hydrography not matching a newer orthoimage. Customers most often expressed that data quality was a concern when they observed examples where elevation and hydrography were not properly aligned on a map. While this was a test of cartographic quality, the implications for geospatial analysis are significant.

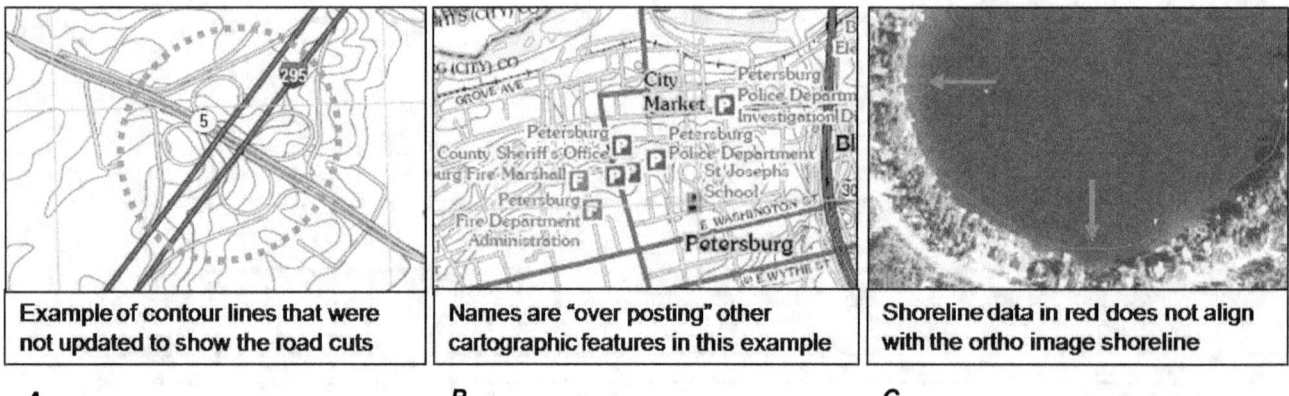

| Example of contour lines that were not updated to show the road cuts | Names are "over posting" other cartographic features in this example | Shoreline data in red does not align with the ortho image shoreline |

A.   *B.*   *C.*

Figure 5.   Maps and orthoimage showing (*A*) contour lines that were not updated to show roadcuts, (*B*) names over posting other features, and (*C*) shoreline data that do not align with the orthoimage shoreline. Customers were more tolerant of contours that have not been updated for a transportation feature cut and fill when compared to contour and hydrography conflicts. Cartographic over posting and shorelines that do not match an orthoimage were more acceptable than other kinds of errors.

access to geospatial data more highly than viewing or other mapping services. More specifically, as shown in table 13, when customers were asked to rank geospatial services, the need to download data ranked more highly than other services.

Customers were asked to rate a number of services offered by the USGS and more generally about their use of commercial, State, and local government services. Generally, the commercial, State, and local services rated more highly than USGS services (see table 14). In the ASPRS survey, which has more representation from the commercial sector, the USGS seamless server was more often rated as an important service offering than *The National Map* viewer. It should be noted that while the National Atlas of the United States® (2009) ranked lower than might be anticipated, the target audience for that service is the K–12 educational community and casual users who were not represented in this survey.

The interview team was able to ask followup questions during the interviews. *The National Map* viewer rated lower than other services because customers found it difficult to find the data they needed, and the viewer application was deemed to be too slow and difficult to use. The lack of "seamless" data was viewed as a major obstacle. For those who were very knowledgeable about USGS services, the seamless server was often cited as a useful tool. Unfortunately, many people did not know it existed. In contrast, customers liked the ease of use offered by the commercial services, even though they

often cited the poorer quality data from some of these services as an issue. The user interface and the ability to easily access Keyhole Markup Language (KML) services from Google were the often cited benefits of this ubiquitous service. In addition, the commercial services were viewed as a better venue to distribute information to consumer audiences.

The ESRI survey asked GIS users how often they used USGS services (see table 15). A relatively small portion of the services were used by that user community more than occasionally. The ESRI user survey had a larger response from the local government community than either the structured interviews or the ASPRS survey. As expected, a summary of use by local government compared to all other users clearly showed a significantly lower use rate of USGS map services among local governments.

Customers were asked how often they used various USGS services. Table 16 shows a summary of service usage for five of *The National Map* online services. The response choices provided in the ESRI survey were slightly different from choices given for the structured interview question and the ASPRS survey. The ESRI choices were daily, weekly, monthly, rarely, and never. The structured interviews and the ASPRS survey choices were daily, weekly, monthly, yearly, and don't use. Any usage of these services on a monthly basis would be considered significant because customers often access USGS data for the purpose of making a copy for use

Table 13. Customer ratings of geospatial product and service needs to meet mission-critical requirements.

[A higher mean response is more important. *N,* number of participant responses. Source: USGS interview question 23, ASPRS survey question 15.3]

| Selected products and services | Structured interviews | | ASPRS survey | |
5 - very important, 4 - quite important, 3 - somewhat important, 2 - not very important, 1 - do not use	N	Mean	N	Mean
Geospatial data file download/transfer service	143	4.43	218	4.37
Web feature service or Web coverage service	144	4.09	214	3.86
Online map viewing service	144	4.01	217	3.71
Pre-formatted digital maps for download and printing	142	3.54	212	3.55
Printed maps	143	3.51	222	3.47

Table 14. Customer ratings of Web services relative to their business requirements.

[The viewer for the National Atlas of the United States® targets a consumer audience and has received high ratings from those groups. Commercial services were preferred by customers primarily because of superior usability and performance. *N,* number of participant responses. Source: USGS interview question 24, ASPRS survey question 15.4]

| Web services | Structured interviews | | ASPRS survey | |
5 - very important, 4 - quite important, 3 - somewhat important, 2 - not very important, 1 - do not use	N	Mean	N	Mean
Google Maps/Google Earth, Microsoft TerraServer	143	3.81	191	3.76
State map viewer/services	143	3.38	189	3.56
County/city map viewers	144	3.24	191	3.43
Geographic Names Information System (GNIS)	105	3.01	194	2.76
USGS seamless server	137	3.00	209	3.52
Geospatial One-Stop	139	2.58	203	2.89
National Atlas of the United States®	141	2.53	202	2.85
The National Map viewer	139	2.40	186	2.91

within their respective organizations. The number of respondents from the USGS structured interviews is small because this question solicited a more open ended response in all of the early interviews. The question was later changed to solicit more quantifiable responses.

Customers were asked to rate the importance of new services or capabilities that could be considered for future generations of *The National Map* (see table 17). Access to historical geospatial data was ranked highly by participants in both the structured interviews and the ASPRS survey. More detailed information about historical data needs is found in table 5. Other highly ranked capabilities included enhancements to national datasets that improved their usability for advanced analysis. These included addresses linked to streets and structures, permanent identifiers associated with all geospatial features, and nationwide transportation routes. A primary need to improve data integration includes the requirement to associate data in external datasets to *The National Map*. Each of these capabilities would allow for more effective use of online Web services by supporting improved mechanisms to link services.

Customer Requirements—Topographic Maps

The USGS is developing the capability to update and publish new orthoimage and topographic maps. These are digital products that are derived from an enterprise database composed of eight geospatial data themes to include orthoimagery, transportation, hydrography, elevation, names, land cover, boundaries, and structures. A number of approaches have been considered for meeting production objectives. Generally, the approaches under review require that customer input on content completeness, data quality, and production rates be taken into consideration. While it is desirable to produce the highest quality maps in the largest numbers, it is recognized that a national program of this scope must consider the tradeoffs between these variables to find the most cost-effective solution to meet the greatest needs. Customers were asked a series of questions about their reliance on maps,

how they created them, and their utility in the day of advanced geospatial systems technology.

Customers were asked how important USGS topographic maps were to the mission-related work in their organizations. Nearly 60 percent of the surveyed organizations said that they were quite important or very important (see table 18). When customers indicating that they were somewhat important are considered, about 80 percent of all respondents said that USGS topographic maps were important to their organizations. The customers interviewed by the USGS said that they used the topographic maps as a printed product about half of the time (see table 19). The ASPRS survey membership community indicated that field use was a smaller component of the overall usage at about 35 percent. Regardless, the printed map is still viewed as an important product. A number of questions about printing, print format, and printing costs were asked to determine how to best respond to this need.

Customers were presented with a list of geospatial data layers that could potentially be displayed on a topographic map and asked to rate their importance (see table 20). This was a nearly identical list to the question that was asked from a data perspective earlier (table 5) except that customers were asked about their need to have a woodland tint displayed on the topographic map rather than the land cover dataset that was listed under the list of data types needed to support geospatial analysis in their organizations. These data types related to the existing USGS list of map data types found on a printed USGS topographic map.

While the USGS may have a requirement to have access to all of these datasets, under the auspices of the Office of Management and Budget (OMB, 2002) Circular A–16, the USGS has management responsibilities for hydrography, orthoimagery, elevation, geographic names, and land cover. On the basis of input from customers on their requirements for map content, the USGS priorities could be established to focus on those datasets with the greatest defined need. The highest priority datasets include transportation (public roads), hydrography, elevation, orthoimagery, geographic names, boundaries (city, county, State, international), and the Public Land Survey

Table 15.   Customer ratings of Web service—ESRI survey.

[Customer response average for a selection of USGS geospatial services. The percent favorable response is based on the number of customers who selected either daily, weekly, or monthly usage. When compared to other users, local government customers had a significantly lower use of USGS services: Source: ESRI survey question 7]

USGS online services - frequency of use	ESRI survey - All respondents			ESRI survey - Local government only			ESRI survey - TOTAL without local government		
5 - daily, 4 - weekly, 3 - monthly, 2 - rarely, 1 - never	Average	Percent Favorable	Total	Average	Percent Favorable	Total	Average	Percent Favorable	Total
Geospatial One-Stop	2.20	34%	1558	1.85	19%	496	2.36	41%	1062
The National Map seamless server	2.19	34%	1566	1.82	18%	496	2.36	41%	1070
The National Map viewer	2.15	32%	1569	1.87	20%	500	2.28	37%	1069
Geographic Names Information System (GNIS)	2.13	30%	1561	1.79	17%	498	2.30	36%	1063
National Atlas of the United States®	2.10	29%	1557	1.78	15%	498	2.25	36%	1059
The National Hydrography Dataset (NHD) viewer	2.04	27%	1555	1.71	15%	494	2.19	33%	1061
Maps on Demand	1.91	21%	1558	1.73	13%	498	1.99	25%	1060
The USGS store	1.88	19%	1560	1.70	11%	496	1.96	22%	1064

Table 16.   Side-by-side comparison of *The National Map* (TNM) service usage.

[List is sorted by the cross sample average, which gives equal ranking to each of the three data collection activities. Structured interview sample of 45 represents the number of interviews conducted where this question was asked. Early interviewees were asked a more general question about which services customers used. *N*, number of participant responses. Source: USGS interview question 5, ASPRS survey question 15.2, ESRI survey question 7]

TNM online services	Cross sample average	Weighted average	Structured interviews					ASPRS survey					ESRI survey				
			Monthly	Weekly	Daily	N	Total percent	Monthly	Weekly	Daily	N	Total percent	Monthly	Weekly	Daily	N	Total percent
The National Map seamless server	40.3%	35 80%	20.0%	6.7%	11.1%	45	37.8%	30.7%	15.4%	3 5%	254	49.6%	21.1%	9.7%	2.7%	1566	33 5%
Geographic Names Information System (GNIS)	37.1%	30 88%	20.0%	6.7%	20.0%	45	46.7%	21.7%	8.8%	4.4%	249	34.9%	19 6%	7.7%	2 5%	1561	29 8%
The National Map viewer	34.0%	33 20%	17.8%	2.2%	6.7%	45	26.7%	31 0%	11.1%	1 6%	252	43.7%	22 2%	7 8%	1.7%	1569	31.7%
The National Hydrography Dataset (NHD) viewer	31.6%	27.43%	17.8%	13.3%	8.9%	45	40.0%	19.4%	7 3%	1 2%	247	27.9%	18 6%	6.4%	2 0%	1555	27.0%
The USGS store	26.1%	20 27%	20.0%	2.2%	11.1%	45	33.3%	19 6%	5 3%	1 2%	245	26.1%	15 8%	2 8%	0.4%	1560	19.0%

Table 17.   New services or capabilities that could be provided by *The National Map*.

[Average rating of new services or capabilities that could be considered for *The National Map* in the future. Highest rated capabilities included access to historical data and a suite of capabilities to link other datasets to *The National Map* data layers. *N*, number of participant responses. Source: USGS interview question 25, ASPRS survey question 15.5]

Other advanced products, services	Structured interviews		ASPRS survey	
5 - very important, 4 - quite important, 3 - somewhat important, 2 - not very important, 1 - not important at all	N	Mean	N	Mean
Historical geospatial data retention	143	3.69	200	3.53
Nationwide addresses linked to streets and/or structures	145	3.66	210	3.49
Permanent IDs on all features	144	3.61	200	3.09
Nationwide transportation routes	145	3.57	209	3.65
Advanced integrated data models	143	3.45	202	3.39
Mobile device application or mapping services	143	3.42	204	3.25
Application toolkit for value added use of data or services	143	3.15	199	3.08
Geospatial features with cartographic offsets for improved maps	143	3.13	201	3.05
Nationwide transportation mileposts	144	2.79	204	2.76
Citizen volunteer contributions to *The National Map*	144	2.60	198	2.47
3D fly across the United States	144	2.56	208	2.56

Table 18.   Importance of USGS topographic maps to mission-related work within surveyed organizations.

[Response was evaluated on a five-point scale, where 5 was equal to very important use. *N*, number of participant responses. Source: USGS interview question 7, ASPRS survey question 8.2)]

Use of digital or printed USGS topographic maps	Interviews		ASPRS survey	
	N	Percent	N	Percent
Very important (5)	59	39.3%	84	29.6%
Quite important (4)	27	18.0%	82	28.9%
Somewhat important (3)	30	20.0%	64	22.5%
Not very important (2)	21	14.0%	29	10.2%
I don't use them (1)	13	8.7%	25	8.8%
Total	150		284	
Percent very or quite important		57.3%		58.5%
Mean		3.65		3.60

System (see table 20). In addition, the ASPRS survey of its predominantly commercial service sector membership recognized the high level of importance for vertical and horizontal control.

The USGS has evaluated a number of commercial datasets for use on published topographic and orthoimage maps. In all cases, a license places some restrictions on how the data are used or can be made available to customers of *The National Map*. While use of commercial datasets may be a cost-effective way to meet the map publishing objectives, these licensed datasets in the enterprise geospatial database carry use restrictions. About half of the customers find these limitations to be important or very important issues to their organizations (see table 21). If a "somewhat important" response is also considered, then about 70 percent of the customers find these limitations to be problematic.

While the question was not specifically asked, the interview teams learned in the structured interviews that customers want to see the same data regardless of the product form in which it is distributed. For example, if the USGS publishes a topographic map of an area, *The National Map* viewer should be displaying the same data, and the download service should distribute the digital data as represented on the published map as well. To use data with any restrictions, regardless of the product, would mean that the USGS must support multiple datasets for the same themes and that the common source objective could not be met. This should not be interpreted to mean that commercial datasets cannot be used in *The National Map*. It may be possible to acquire data from a commercial provider under a public use license that either is lower resolution or supports reduced functionality. If a vendor is willing to make available some baseline components of their data for unrestricted use, there could also be value that is derived by the vendor in the form of added services to the user community.

Printing technologies for the USGS topographic map required that "separates" be created to coincide with each color represented on a printed map. For many years, the USGS responded to customer requests to reproduce these stable base separates to support customer map production and printing needs. Today, color separations can be created from the database but more importantly, digital printing processes have effectively eliminated this requirement. Customers confirmed this assertion by a nearly unanimous positive response to the USGS structured interview question 28 about separations.

A scenario was created to assess the customer priorities for quality tradeoffs and topographic map production rates. The hypothetical scenario asked the customer to select either a high production rate and a corresponding lower quality or a lower production rate in exchange for higher quality. Customers were willing to compromise quality if they had the ability to identify a subset of the maps that would be created to a higher standard. The responses to the structured interviews and the ASPRS survey are shown in table 22. For the ESRI survey, the scenario provided an option to select lower levels of feature richness and integration as a means to improve production rates. When asked in this way, 60 percent of the customers said that would be acceptable.

The procedures for creating a digital topographic map are fully automated and can be implemented either to publish on demand or to publish and stage premade maps for download. There are benefits and drawbacks to each approach, and a scenario was created to assess customer preferences. While either approach is feasible, production planning and database development will be influenced by the approach that is ultimately selected for the initial digital rollout product. Customers were asked to select either the option to download a premade map immediately or the option to create a new map (with the latest data) in 20 minutes. Most customers wanted to have the option of doing either, but when forced to make a decision, an equal number picked premade and publish on demand. This equal split was true for both the structured interviews and the ASPRS survey. In discussions during the interview, most

Table 19.   Use of printed versus digital forms of topographic maps.

[Customers were allowed to check multiple uses, and so the detailed responses (*N*) total more than the number of customers who indicated that they used topographic maps. Source: USGS interview question 6, ASPRS survey question 8.1]

Use of topographic maps	Interviews		ASPRS survey	
	N	Percent	*N*	Percent
Use them in one or more ways described in detail below	117	84.8%	247	88.2%
Don't use topographic maps	21	15.2%	33	11.8%
Total	138		280	
Detail	*N*	Percent	*N*	Percent
Primarily as a printed product	67	48.6%	98	35.0%
Primarily as a stand alone digital product on a laptop or handheld computer	45	32.6%	72	25.7%
Primarily as a digital product on a laptop or handheld computer with additional data display, data entry, or markup and editing capability	74	53.6%	138	49.3%
Other	21	15.2%	15	5.4%

Table 20.   Required geospatial data layers to be displayed or printed on a topographic map.

[Customers were required to force rank 7 low, 7 medium, and 7 high data layers. *N*, number of participant responses. Source: USGS interview question 10, ASPRS survey question 10.1]

Geospatial data layers displayed on a map	Structured interview				ASPRS survey			
		Percent				Percent		
	N	Low	Medium	High	N	Low	Medium	High
Transportation - Public streets/roads	119	6%	9%	85%	254	5%	15%	80%
Hydrography – Surface water	116	4%	19%	77%	250	12%	28%	60%
Elevation	119	6%	23%	71%	251	8%	16%	77%
Orthoimagery	113	25%	18%	58%	256	10%	14%	76%
Geographic names	116	10%	38%	53%	247	22%	41%	38%
Boundaries – city, county, state, international	119	9%	41%	50%	251	17%	36%	47%
Boundaries - Public Land Survey System	117	31%	27%	43%	248	32%	30%	38%
Physiographic feature names (mountain, plain, etc)	114	33%	34%	33%	250	39%	38%	22%
Boundaries – Federal and Na ive American lands	118	28%	41%	31%	242	44%	34%	22%
Parcels	116	49%	22%	28%	250	45%	26%	28%
Pipelines and powerlines	117	30%	43%	27%	248	36%	41%	23%
Structures – public (e.g. schools, hospitals)	118	36%	37%	26%	244	35%	40%	25%
Vertical and horizontal control	119	34%	40%	26%	250	32%	23%	45%
Transportation – Other routes e.g. forest roads	119	37%	40%	24%	246	51%	35%	14%
Transportation – Trails	119	35%	44%	22%	246	46%	40%	15%
Springs and wells	117	48%	32%	21%	240	59%	29%	13%
Transportation – Railroads	119	31%	49%	20%	250	26%	46%	28%
Transportation – Airports	118	35%	47%	19%	247	32%	42%	27%
Vegetation – woodland tint (subset of land cover)	115	31%	50%	18%	251	30%	44%	26%
Structures – rural areas	118	43%	42%	14%	240	54%	34%	12%
Structures – Urban area designation (tint)	117	37%	51%	12%	242	38%	44%	18%

Table 21.   Customer sensitivity to data use limits through license restrictions.

[A "very important" response indicates that any restrictions would be unacceptable for the customer. Source: USGS interview question 26, ASPRS survey question 16.1]

Sensitivity to use (license) restrictions	Structured interviews		ASPRS survey	
	Frequency	Percent	Frequency	Percent
Minimal	13	11.3%	38	18.2%
Not very important	15	13.0%	33	15.8%
Somewhat important	25	21.7%	50	23.9%
Important	27	23.5%	38	18.2%
Very important	35	30.4%	50	23.9%
Total	115		209	

Table 22.   Response to topographic map production scenarios.

[Response to production scenario where customer selected one of three quality-versus-quantity alternatives. *N*, number of participant responses. Source: USGS interview question 29, ASPRS survey question 16.4]

Quality versus timeliness tradeoff	Structured interviews		ASPRS survey	
	N	Percent	N	Percent
55K quads in 10 yrs (highest quality)	43	37.1%	75	38.7%
55K quads in 3 yrs (lower quality)	20	17.2%	46	23.7%
10K high quality quads and 45K lower quality quads in 5 yrs	53	45.7%	73	37.6%
Total	116		194	

customers felt that with today's technology, this choice should not be an issue.

A followup question to the publish-on-demand scenario was asked to determine which online mapping features would be most important to topographic map users. Five basic capabilities were presented as shown in table 23. The two most important capabilities identified by customers included publishing a map with a user-identified map center and picking and choosing geospatial data layers. This result is significant in that it suggests that a publish-on-demand capability would be more favorably received since staging finished maps in a digital repository is not possible if the customer wishes to select the map center. The planned published topographic map product will have the capability to support layering and printing functions and can be supported as either the publish-on-demand scenario or the select-and-download approach.

Most existing USGS topographic maps are published on the North American Datum of 1927 (NAD 27) and do not have full Universal Transverse Mercator/U.S. National Grid (UTM/USNG) lines. Customers were asked if the change in datum and grid lines on newer products would create any operational problems for their organizations (see table 24). The concern is that users may be confused by multiple grids on a single map or older maps showing different grids or that in some situations, coordinate values might be used in one grid system but reported in another. This datum change was deemed to be a significant problem for about 25 percent of the interview and survey participants. The project team hypothesized that this was a problem that most significantly impacted the emergency response community. While this may be a factor, a more in depth analysis indicated that a wide range of organizations are potentially impacted by this problem. The change in datum and grid representation is not unique to *The National Map*. It is likely that the datum and grid line changes will need to be widely communicated through education and outreach by the USGS and other organizations because there is no good solution short of republishing every map in existence.

Customers were asked two different questions about their willingness to pay for a printed topographic map (see tables 25, 26). Currently the costs for commercial printing of large (24 inch by 30 inch) documents range from about $25 to $35 and higher for special media. The USGS currently offers a print-on-demand service for copies of topographic map products that are out of print. While the established price to a customer is relatively low for the print-on-demand service, it is significantly subsidized to be more consistent with the price of in-stock, high-volume-printed topographic maps. Customers with professional GIS staff and systems overwhelmingly said that they would provide for their own printing needs and that a $35 per map price was simply too high. Neither the interviews nor the ASPRS survey directly targeted the many consumers who use a significant number of topographic maps. It is expected that the critical price point for this group would also be below $10 (see table 25). An interesting observation is that the professionals who responded to the question about

online functionality (table 23) did not rate home printing or maps designed for standard printers very highly. It is likely that they either didn't grasp the significance of the question or they felt that their needs could easily be met by internal plotting capability.

Customers have specialized needs for printed products (see table 27). While the formal questions asked did not specifically address the business drivers, it was learned through discussion during the interviews that printed maps that will hold up to the rigors of field use are very important. Desires for durability include paper that will not fall apart in the rain and ink that will not run or wash out in the sun. Other customers have requirements to maintain archival quality maps, and longevity was their primary concern. These organizations generally take care of their own printing needs, and the proposed digital product was an acceptable solution for them.

A new geo-referenced topographic map product was described to customers as an item that could be distributed as a GeoPDF or a tagged image file format (TIFF) product and could be downloaded from a map-on-demand Internet application. It would also support the ability to overlay customer data. The customer was then asked if a plotted output instead of a lithographic print would be an acceptable product to be generated from the digital file (see table 28). A large majority of customers indicated that this would be an acceptable product and that they were willing to give up the lithographic printed paper product.

One feature under consideration for the geo-referenced topographic map product is a "mark up" capability that would allow map users to digitally mark maps with attribute or spatial updates. While in the field, a worker could mark updates on the map and later display or download these updates to a GIS where they could be further utilized to support updates or to meet other business needs. More than 75 percent of the customers agreed that this was an important or very important capability (see table 29). Customers often asked additional questions during the interviews because they didn't fully understand either the capabilities or the limits of the new functionality. After further discussion, it was apparent that there was significant interest but that users needed to be better informed about the product.

A green tint representing vegetation has always been a recognizable feature of a topographic map. Sometimes, the USGS topographic map is referred to as the green map. The source of data for the green layer in a modern topographic map has been under study, and it is likely that this layer will be derived from the National Land Cover Dataset (NLCD). The NLCD is a Landsat satellite derived product and as such does not meet the spatial accuracy requirements of a published 1:24000-scale USGS topographic map. Customers were shown sample map images (fig. 6) and asked if they had requirements for the vegetation layer that would preclude the use of these medium-resolution datasets. About 75 percent of the customers indicated that this would be an acceptable practice, and less than 10 percent indicated that it would not be acceptable at all.

Table 23. Online mapping features for publish-on-demand technology.

[*N*, number of participant responses. Source: USGS interview question 31, ASPRS survey question 16.6]

Online mapping features	Structured interviews				ASPRS survey	
1 - highest importance to 5 - lowest importance	*N*	Average rank	Min.	Max.	*N*	Average rank
Select the area of interest to be the center of the map	111	1.83	1	5	180	2.23
Pick and choose layers to be printed	112	2.04	1	5	177	2.07
Control the print scale	111	2.80	1	5	175	2.34
Select multiple formats such as letter or legal with map frames for each format	111	3.73	1	5	186	3.71
Tile a standard 7.5 minute quad for printing on a home printer	109	4.49	1	5	194	4.18

Table 24. Use of different datum and grid lines on older series topographic maps.

[New published USGS map products use different datum and grid lines than shown on older series maps, most of which use the North American Datum of 1927 (NAD 27). This question assessed how problematic that might be to customers. *N*, number of participant responses. Source: USGS interview question 32, ASPRS survey question 16.7]

Difficulty using old maps with NAD 27 datum and new maps with different datum and grid lines	Structured interviews		ASPRS survey	
	N	Percent	*N*	Percent
This is a significant problem, preventing mission-critical operations	32	28.1%	53	25.9%
This is a problem, but only in small ways or in unusual circumstances	45	39.5%	92	44.9%
This is not a problem. Our work doesn't depend on printed grids and coordinates	37	32.5%	60	29.3%
Total	114		205	

Table 25. Customer willingness to pay for a printed topographic map.

[Price points identifying customer willingness to pay for a printed topographic map. *N*, number of participant responses. Source: USGS interview question 33, ASPRS survey question 17.1]

Map price and willingness to pay	Structured interview		ASPRS survey	
	N	Percent	*N*	Percent
$0	60	51.3%	103	50.7%
$10	37	31.6%	72	35.5%
$15	9	7.7%	9	4.4%
$20	6	5.1%	10	4.9%
$25	4	3.4%	1	0.5%
$30	0	0.0%	1	0.5%
$35	1	0.9%	7	3.4%
Total	117		203	

Table 26. Assessment of customer willingness to use a commercial service for printing if the print cost were $35 per map sheet.

[*N*, number of participant responses. Source: USGS interview question 34, ASPRS survey question 17.2]

Willingness to pay a vendor such as FedEx Kinkos $35 for a typical 24" x 30" map product	Structured interview		ASPRS survey	
	N	Percent	*N*	Percent
Yes, this is a good option for me	7	5.8%	15	7.2%
No, my organization could print these in-house and we usually would	100	83.3%	160	76.9%
No, we seldom or never use printed maps	13	10.8%	33	15.9%
Total	120		208	

Table 27.   Customer requirements for special topographic map print media.

[Customer requirements for special print media to include dimensionally stable paper and waterproof inks. *N*, number of participant responses. Source: USGS interview question 35, ASPRS survey question 17.3]

Need for printed maps on special media	Structured interviews		ASPRS survey	
	N	Percent	*N*	Percent
Not important at all	27	22.9%	40	19.3%
Not very important	29	24.6%	70	33.8%
Somewhat important	43	36.4%	59	28.5%
Very important	19	16.1%	38	18.4%
Total	118		207	

Table 28.   Customer satisfaction with topographic map digital product versus a lithographic print.

[Customers agreed that a digital product was an acceptable alternative to a lithographic print. *N*, number of participant responses. Source: USGS interview question 37, ASPRS survey question 17.5]

Proposal to discontinue lithographic printing in favor of digital product	Structured interviews		ASPRS survey	
	N	Percent	*N*	Percent
Completely satisfied with this approach	71	59.7%	91	45.3%
Generally satisfied with this approach	36	30.3%	87	43.3%
Somewhat satisfied, I occasionally need lithographic prints	9	7.6%	15	7.5%
Dissatisfied, I need lithographic prints regularly	3	2.5%	8	4.0%
Total	119		201	

Table 29.   Customer assessment of digital "mark up" capability on a published map product.

[Customers liked the concept of a digital "mark up" capability on a published map product but were unsure of how they would fully utilize this functionality. *N*, number of participant responses. Source: USGS interview question 28, ASPRS survey question 17.6]

Digital "mark up" support on published map	Structured interviews		ASPRS survey	
	N	Percent	*N*	Percent
Very important feature, I would use it regularly	45	38.1%	72	36.0%
Important feature	51	43.2%	81	40.5%
Only somewhat important feature	19	16.1%	38	19.0%
Unimportant feature, I would seldom use it	3	2.5%	9	4.5%
Total	118		200	

Vegetation and urban "tint" image on left was created from the National Land Cover Dataset medium-resolution data. The photo and topographic map images are for reference only.

Figure 6.   Image showing green tint derived from Landsat satellite data to test the concept that not all data layers need to meet the same level of precision on published map products. Source: USGS interview question 40, ASPRS survey question 22.1.

A number of topographic map production scenarios are under consideration at the USGS, thus prompting a question about feature richness on published map products. Two graphics (fig. 7) were shown to customers where one showed the name and airport runway configuration, and the other simply showed an airport symbol and the name. The question also indicated that pipelines, powerlines, springs, and wells may or may not be shown on published maps. About 60 percent of the respondents to both the structured interviews and the ASPRS survey responded favorably to the idea that content may vary from map to map (see table 30). During interviews, however, some customers felt strongly that some features such as hospitals and police stations should be represented uniformly on all maps. In addition, customers wanted to be assured that there was a long-term plan for bringing all maps to a uniform standard.

While a topographic map is assumed to have some representation of elevation or topographic relief, there are many ways to display this on a map. Customers were presented with four options (fig. 8) that might be used in future topographic map products and asked to identify their preferred standard display preference. In both the structured interviews and the ASPRS survey, there was a strong preference for the two examples that displayed the contour lines (see table 31). Customers felt that the option to see shaded relief with elevation "bands" was pleasing to look at but was not sufficient to serve the need to have contours on the map. The example in figure 8 that shows land cover combined with topographic relief was difficult to interpret for some people who participated in the interviews.

Today, geospatial data come from many sources, and the map publication date, while important, is a poor indicator of the currency of the underlying datasets. For any individual dataset, the definition of "current" can be highly variable as well. The example metadata reference diagram (fig. 9) was presented to customers to get their feedback on the need for metadata detail to be included on a published map (see table 32). Customers liked the source reference for each data layer but felt that at a minimum, there should also be a date associated with each data layer and that there should be a uniform resource locator (URL) listed where more complete information might be obtained. The need to store publication-relevant metadata online presents a new challenge for *The National Map* because only the current data layer metadata are maintained today. This requirement would indicate that a metadata rollback capability is necessary so that the metadata as of the publication date could be generated on demand. Alternatively, the full date-specific metadata could be published in the GeoPDF topographic product file but could not be maintained by the USGS in a central repository.

Customer Wishes for *The National Map*

To help plan a path for the evolution of *The National Map*, respondents to the USGS structured interviews and the ASPRS survey were asked "If you had three wishes for NEW *The National Map* features, layers, or other functionality within the next three to five years, what would you wish for?" (USGS interview question 16, ASPRS question 12.4). Responses for this question were in free-form text, and so analysis was limited to simple tallies by response type. No additional statistical analysis could be completed. In the ESRI survey, only one wish was asked for, and respondents were

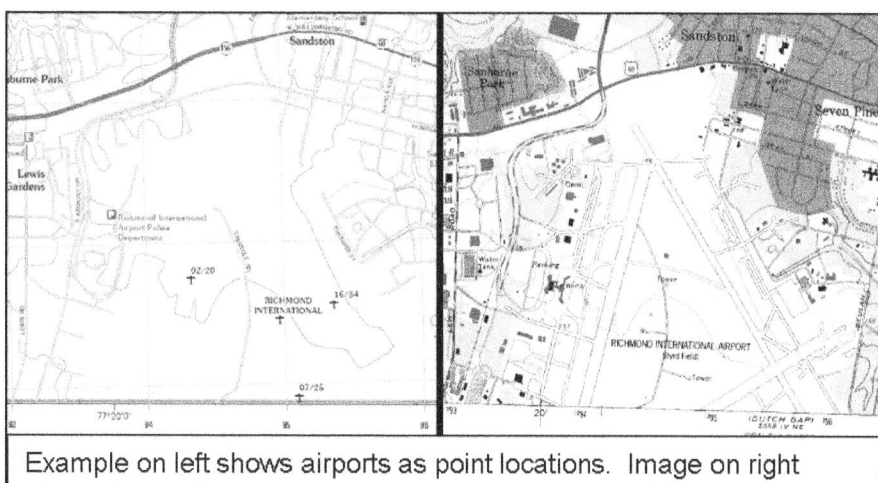

Example on left shows airports as point locations. Image on right shows airport detail.

Figure 7.   Example showing how topographic maps might have variable feature content detail. In this example, the airport runway may or may not be displayed depending on whether or not the data existed in the enterprise database. Source: USGS interview question 41, ASPRS survey question 22.2.

Table 30.   Customer assessment of variable content on topographic maps.

[Customers were asked to respond to the idea that some maps would be published with more features (or data layers) than others. *N*, number of participant responses. Source: USGS interview question 41, ASPRS survey question 22.2]

Some topographic maps would be more feature rich than others	Structured interviews		ASPRS survey	
	N	Percent	N	Percent
4=Very acceptable	24	19.8%	36	18.3%
3=Acceptable	52	43.0%	83	42.1%
2=Not very acceptable	35	28.9%	64	32.5%
1=Not acceptable at all	10	8.3%	14	7.1%
Total	121		197	
Percent favorable (rating 3+4)		62.8%		60.4%

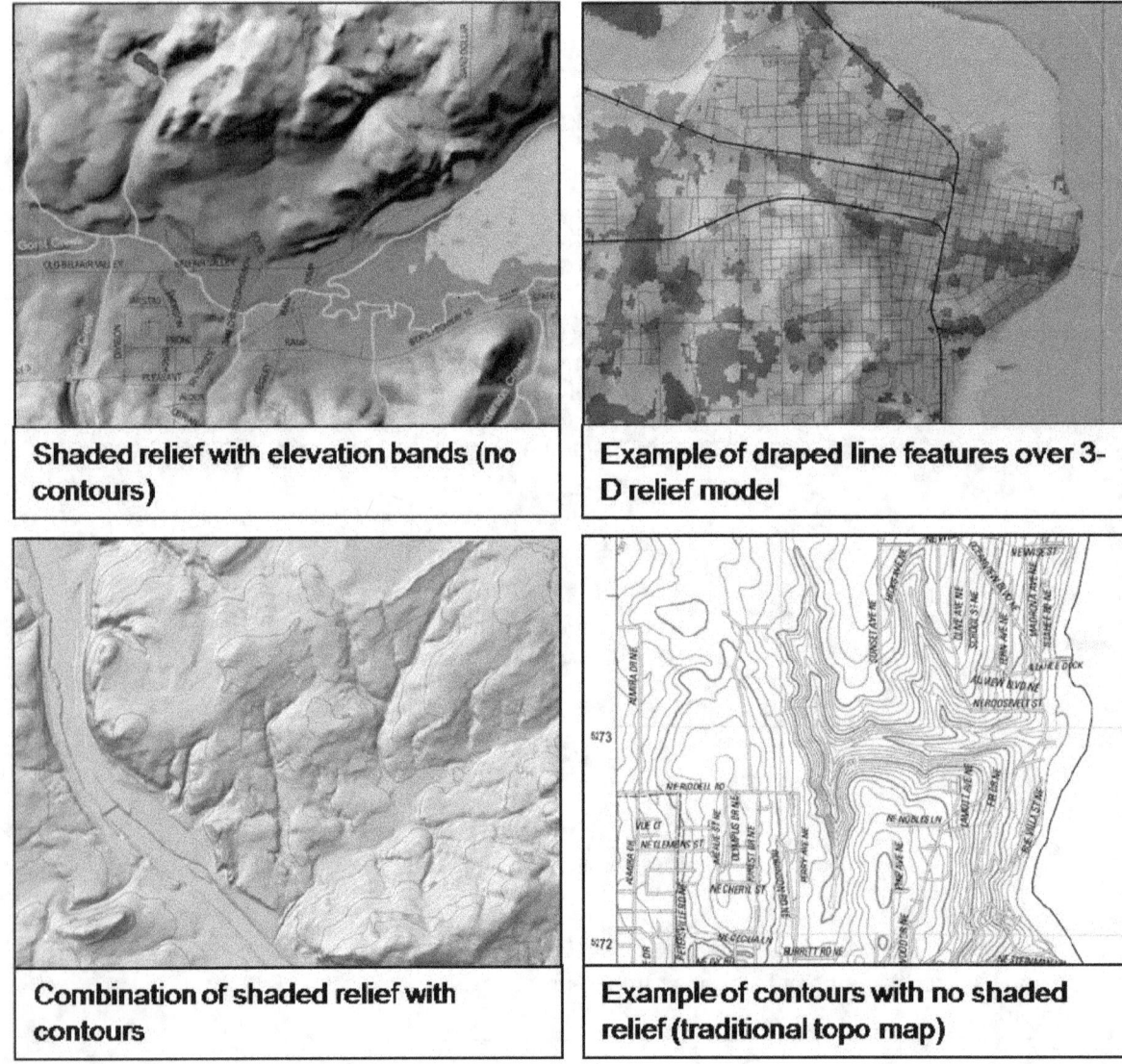

Figure 8.   When customers were presented with prototype views of a published topographic map, they most often picked one of the two lower image samples. Published contours were common to these two examples and were cited as being important for a topographic map. Source: USGS interview question 42, ASPRS survey question 23.1.

Table 31.   Customer assessment of prototype topographic maps with contours and shaded relief.

[Customers strongly preferred topographic maps with contours over maps that only displayed shaded relief. *N*, number of participant responses. Source: USGS interview question 42, ASPRS survey question 23.1]

Customer preference for published topography and relief	Structured interview				ASPRS survey	
	First choice		Second choice		First choice	Second choice
	N	Percent	*N*	Percent	Percent (*N*)	Percent (*N*)
Combination of shaded relief and contours	49	39.5%	41	34.5%	54.7% (70)	45.3% (58)
Contours on digital topo	36	29.0%	34	28.6%	54.6% (59)	45.4% (49)
Shaded relief with elevation color bands	22	17.7%	21	17.6%	44.1% (26)	55.9% (33)
Draping the imagery and line features over a 3-D relief model	9	7.3%	12	10.1%	32.4% (11)	67.6% (23)
Combination of drape with contours (no figure available)	8	6.5%	11	9.2%	49.2% (32)	50.8% (33)
Total	124		119			

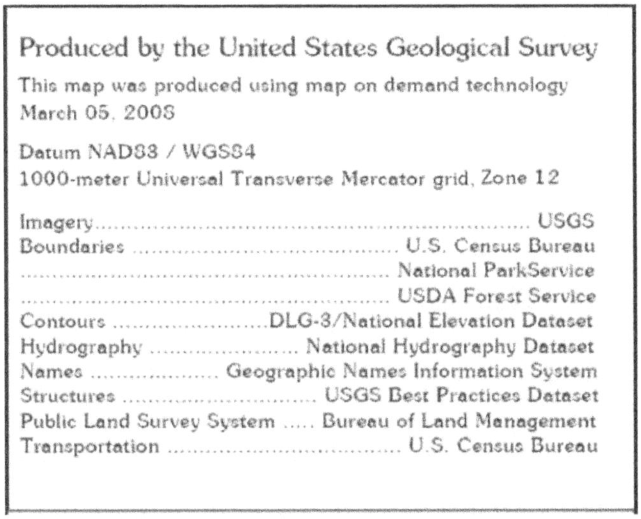

Produced by the United States Geological Survey

This map was produced using map on demand technology March 05, 2008

Datum NAD83 / WGS84
1000-meter Universal Transverse Mercator grid, Zone 12

Imagery.. USGS
Boundaries .... U.S. Census Bureau
.... National ParkService
.... USDA Forest Service
Contours ....DLG-3/National Elevation Dataset
Hydrography .... National Hydrography Dataset
Names .... Geographic Names Information System
Structures .... USGS Best Practices Dataset
Public Land Survey System ..... Bureau of Land Management
Transportation .... U.S. Census Bureau

Figure 9.   Illustration of proposed data source citation to be included in the legend of the published topographic map. Customers requested more detail to include the edit date for each layer and expanded online metadata with URL published on the map. Source: USGS interview question 43, ASPRS survey question 24.1.

asked to elaborate on reasons behind the wish, making those data more time consuming to evaluate (ESRI question 10). With this difference in question format, the ESRI wishes are not directly comparable with responses to the USGS structured interviews and ASPRS survey, and there was no additional analysis on ESRI question 10 done for this report.

Word Frequency Analysis

A text processing engine was used to determine the most frequent words used in each set of responses, leaving out common words such as "and" and "the." Word frequency analysis is a preliminary step in categorizing responses. Important ideas may take the form of value statements; for example, they may include the word "better." These ideas can indicate respondents' attitude but may not fit into a precise category.

The word "data" figures very prominently in both the USGS interview (see fig. 10) and ASPRS survey (see fig. 11) datasets. This result correlates with similar results, discussed above, on ranking which online services (see table 13) are most important to meet customer business needs. Also quite frequent in both datasets are the words "maps," "imagery," and "resolution." The USGS interview text contains many more prominent words relating to institutions, for example, "USGS," "TNM," and "Census," and also words related to data access, for example, "needs," "access," "service," and "available." In the ASPRS dataset, "data" predominates, but not as strongly as in the USGS dataset. More specific datasets are mentioned ("elevation," "parcel") in the ASPRS data, and there is an emphasis on accuracy and currency rather than accessibility. The differences in the distribution of words between the two datasets likely reflect the differences in the population samples of respondents, as the USGS interviews were heavily weighted toward Federal, State, and local government employees, while the ASPRS survey drew responses predominantly from the commercial and academic sectors. These word frequency analyses will help guide questions for

Table 32.   Customer assessment of prototype metadata detail on a topographic map.

[A significant number of customers felt that more metadata detail must be printed on the map and that full metadata need to be accessible for the published map product. *N*, number of participant responses. Source: USGS interview question 43, ASPRS survey question 24.1]

Customer preference for metadata detail on published map	Structured interview		ASPRS survey	
	N	Percent	*N*	Percent
Too much detail	1	0.8%	2	1.0%
Just right	52	43.7%	137	69.5%
Not enough detail	66	55.5%	58	29.4%
Total	119		197	

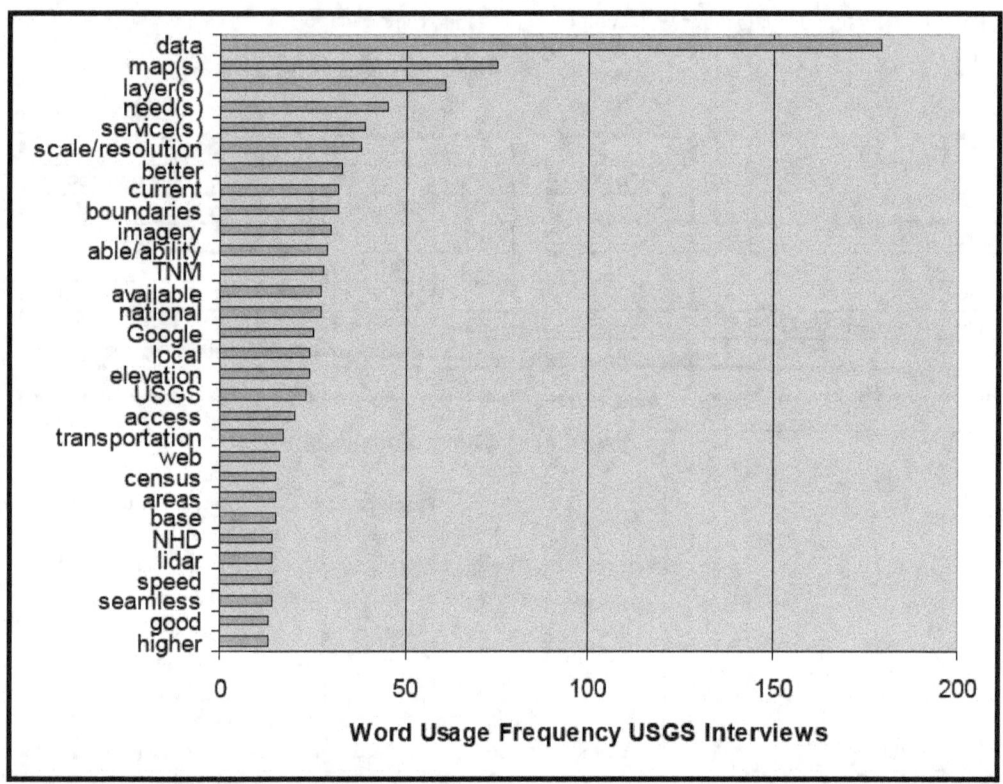

Figure 10.   Frequency of top 30 words in "wishes" responses for USGS structured interview question 16.

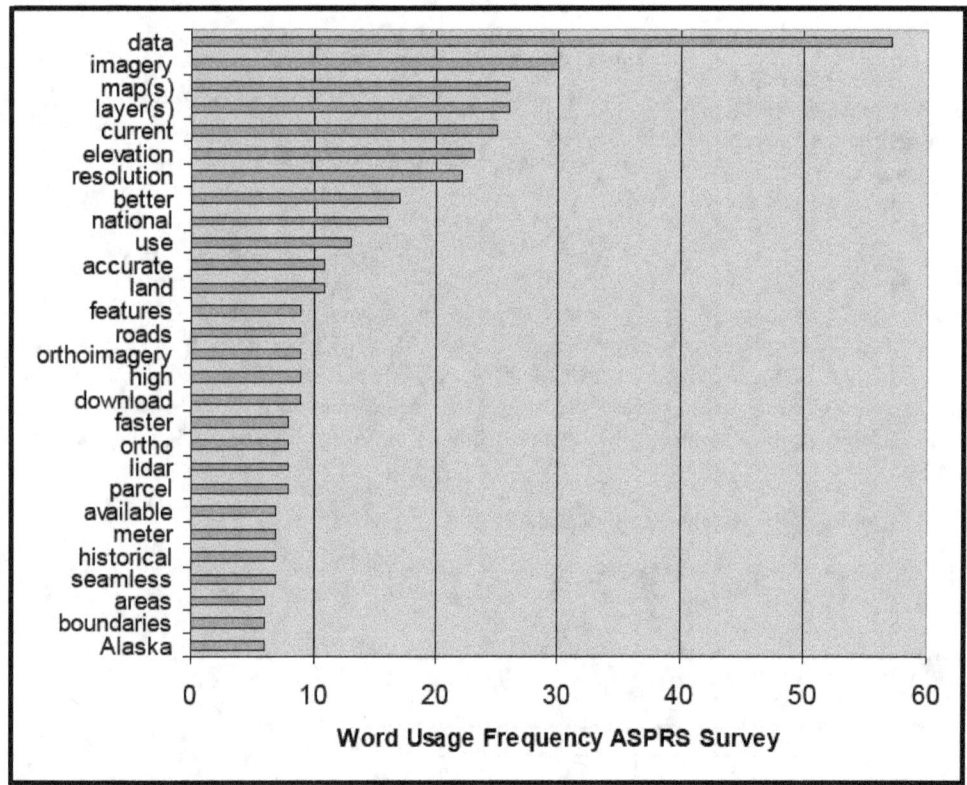

Figure 11.   Frequency of top 30 words in "wishes" responses for ASPRS survey question 12.4.

further sector focus groups. In addition, the structured interviews were normally filled out by the interviewers, and so some consistency in word usage likely occurred, whereas the ASPRS online survey results were completed by the survey participants.

Content Analysis

The content analysis aimed to discover common categories of wishes in the textual answers to the question. Because each respondent could have made up to three wishes, there are more responses than USGS interview or ASPRS survey participants. The USGS interviews produced 430 individual wishes; the ASPRS survey, 314. These wishes (see table 33) could be divided into three broad areas—(1) data of a particular type (such as elevation), (2) general characteristics of data (such as resolution or accuracy), and (3) improvements to the online presence of *The National Map* (such as speed). Historical data were considered a characteristic rather than a data type. Less than 10 percent of the responses in each survey were classified as "other," as they dealt with metadata, digital raster graphics, and printed topographic maps (USGS structured interviews N=37; ASPRS survey N=19). These responses are not a focus of this analysis. Frequently a single response contained more than one idea; for example, a respondent who wished for better elevation data might cite a particular resolution or update frequency. Each of these cited ideas was coded individually, and, in some cases, wishes were cross referenced between wishes about data types and wishes about data characteristics from the same respondent.

Data Types

Datasets or data layers that were specifically mentioned in wishes for the future mirrored the top categories of data appearing in the answers to the question "Please rate the base geospatial data layers in order of importance relative to your organization's business requirements (USGS interview question 9; ASPRS survey question 19)." The highly rated datasets were orthoimagery and imagery, elevation, hydrography, transportation, parcels, and land use, with transportation being more highly rated in the USGS interviews than in the ASPRS survey and land use and land cover being rated lower (fig. 12). These results are somewhat misleading for the elevation

category because LiDAR could have been combined into the elevation category, making elevation the most requested data category. LiDAR has other important uses besides elevation (extraction of building footprints and vegetation, for instance), and so it is categorized below as a separate layer. There were a number of unique types of data mentions (such as biomass, 3-D layers), that did not fit easily into any category. Those were omitted from figure 12.

Data Characteristics

In the content analysis, responses about desired characteristics for data (fig. 13) were divided into seven categories: data integration and data sharing, seamless data that can be clipped out of a dataset and downloaded by a customer, scale or resolution of data, accuracy of data, currency or update frequency of data, need for historical data, and data consistency—referring to standardized data across the Nation.

For the USGS interviewees, the most important future characteristic cited was data integration. Respondents referred to integration not just among different data themes in *The National Map*, but also among data from different organizations whether at Federal, State, or local levels. A typical remark from the USGS interview was "full data integration - if pulling Census, PLSS, etc. info - the data should be vertically integrated and not just thrown together." While integration of themes for which the USGS is a steward may be a highly desirable goal for the USGS to achieve in the next 3 to 5 years, integration of data from other organizations will be more difficult to manage. The ASPRS survey respondents did not mention data integration as often; scale and resolution and currency were more highly valued. A typical comment was "High resolution imagery refreshed every year." The difference in responses to the same question in the USGS interviews and the ASPRS survey, particularly on the integration question, likely reflects the difference in respondent demographics. Federal, State and local government employees who have worked with the USGS and who participated in the structured interviews conducted by the USGS may be more familiar with data sharing and data integration objectives that have been a focus of *The National Map* partnership programs.

Table 33. Wishes for *The National Map*.

[Distribution of wishes (total more than 100 percent). N, number of participant wishes. Source: USGS interview question 12, ASPRS survey question 12.4]

Future wishes	Structured interviews		ASPRS survey	
	N	Percent	*N*	Percent
Data type	229	53%	215	66%
Data characteristics	226	53%	156	50%
Web site function/interface	184	43%	76	24%

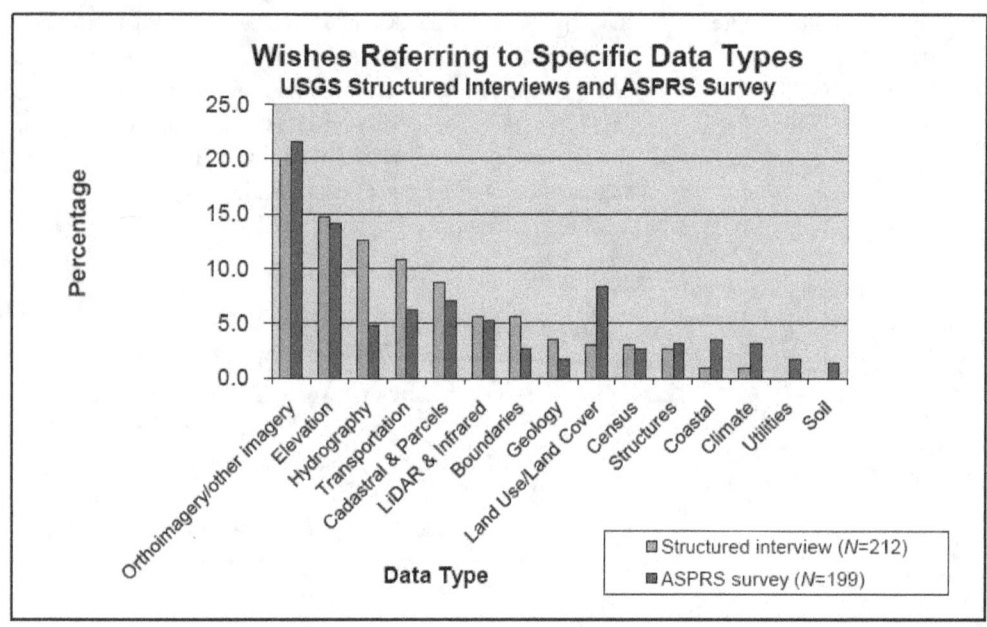

Figure 12.   Wishes referring to specific data types. *N*, number of participant responses. Source: USGS interview question 16, ASPRS survey question 12.4.

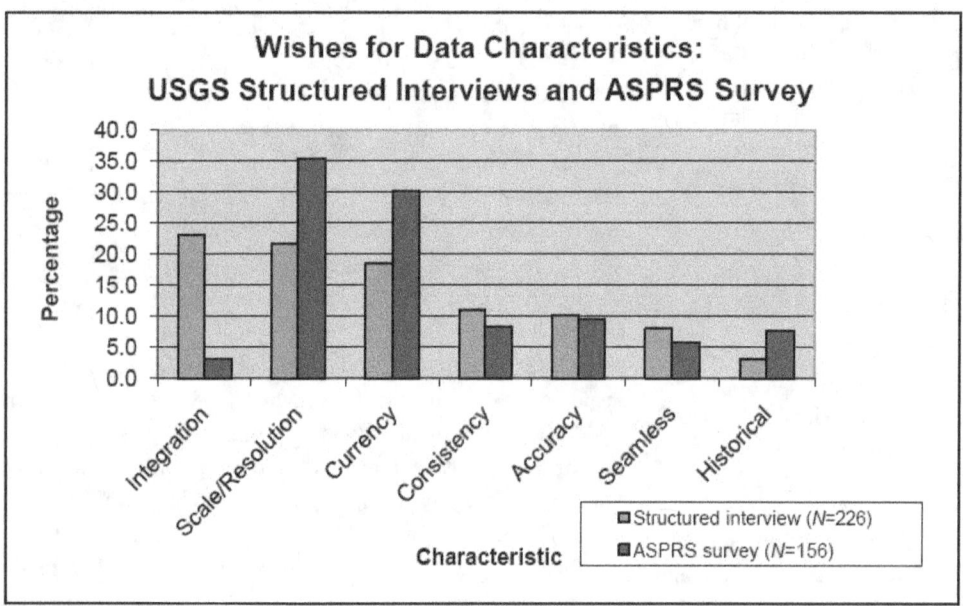

Figure 13.   Wishes for data characteristics. *N*, number of participant responses. Source: USGS interview question 16, ASPRS survey question 12.4.

Wishes about Data Characteristics Associated with Data Types

The top five datasets mentioned in each group of responses were compared to the top three desired data characteristics in each group. For participants in the structured interviews, scale/resolution (fig. 14) was critically important for orthoimagery and elevation. In the ASPRS survey responses (fig. 15), scale was important for elevation, but currency was slightly more important for orthoimagery. In both sets of responses, currency was most important for transportation.

Improvements to Online Presence

Usability and increased functionality of the online mapping system are important to users, particularly for the group

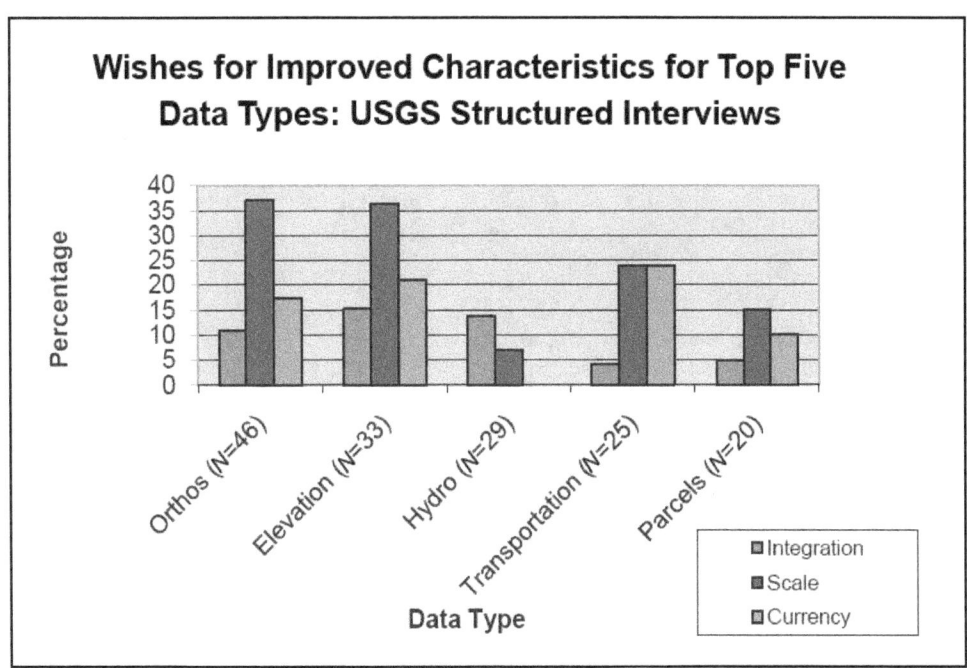

Figure 14. Association of wishes for improved data with data characteristics for top five data types from USGS interview question 16.

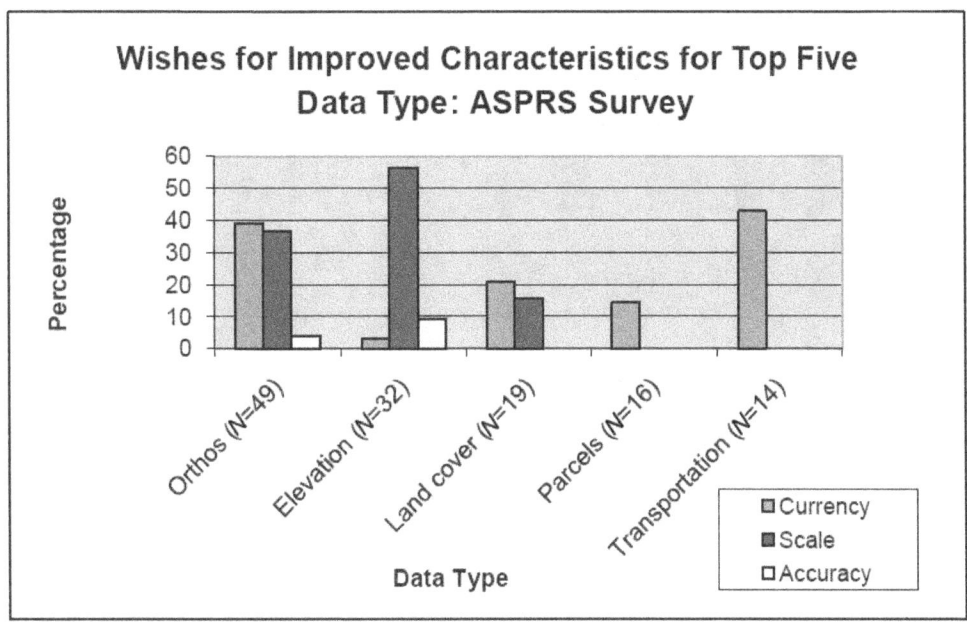

Figure 15. Association of wishes for improved data with data characteristics for top five data types from ASPRS survey question 12.4.

interviewed by the USGS (42 percent of all answers). The responses to both surveys were categorized as follows: ease of use, which included Web site usability, navigation, and improvements to the online map; speed; comparisons to commercial online mapping sites such as Google; and a desire for accessible Web services (fig. 16).

Many respondents from both the USGS structured interviews and the ASPRS survey mentioned that *The National Map* of the future needed to be more like online commercial mapping applications such as Google Maps and Google Earth or Microsoft products:

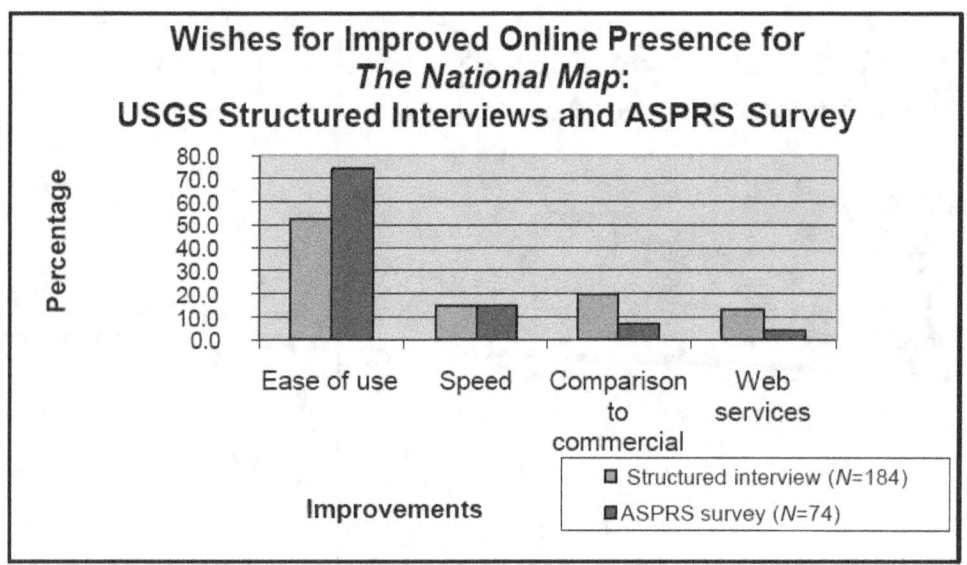

Figure 16.   Wishes for improved online performance for *The National Map*. Source: USGS interview question 16, ASPRS survey question 12.4.

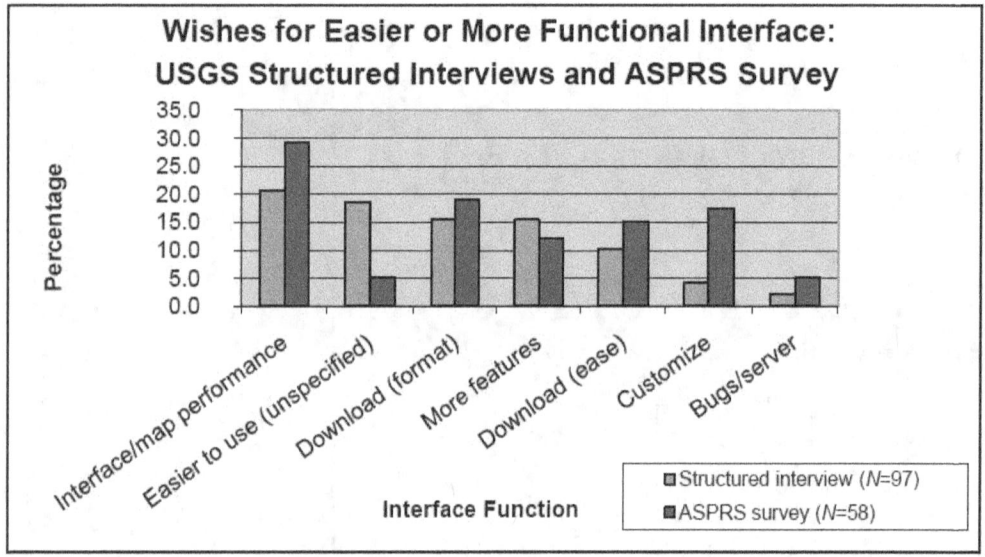

Figure 17.   Wishes for easier or more functional interface. Source: USGS interview question 16, ASPRS survey question 12.4.

National map and seamless should be the same thing, i.e. from a design perspective, Google Earth front end and its speed is what it should be. That front end is phenomenal and all understand it.

This remark from the USGS interviews epitomizes the tone of many of these answers. Not only are these commercial systems seen as speedier and easier, Google and Microsoft, through their open application programming interfaces (API), have given users the ability to interact directly with geospatial databases and create their own maps rather than using pre-made products that might not meet their specific needs:

Features--we need open APIs; we need RSS or an open API that we can build applications on top of it. We do this with Google, but we'd rather have it as a government source to do API and have gold standard is very important.

This is an area where the USGS could provide a critical service because of its reputation for data you can trust ("gold standard"). As one of the USGS interviewees remarked, the USGS has a reputation, a brand: "it must be right because USGS is showing it." As to *The National Map* of the future, many talked about the ability to port data to other devices, to achieve a "mobile national map." This functionality would not only aid hikers and other outdoor enthusiasts who depend on accurate topography, but it would provide a platform for the collection of scientific data for integrated studies in the field via mobile devices.

To get a more nuanced picture of usability issues, the large category "ease of use" was broken down and compared between the USGS structured interviews and the ASPRS survey responses (fig. 17). The new categories were performance of the interface or map, ease of use (not specified), download in formats not currently supported, more features (for example, access to analytical tools), easier download, a customizable viewer or map, and fewer bugs.

In peripheral remarks, most of those interviewed by the USGS indicated that they value the role of the USGS as a national data integrator and would like ongoing opportunities to provide input to the future development of *The National Map*.

Key Findings and Recommendations

Twelve key findings and recommendations are listed under three headings in this section.

Product Need Awareness

1. *Need for nationally consistent data.*—A large majority (88 percent) of all customers from the USGS interviews and the ASPRS survey said that they need data from neighboring jurisdictions or nationally to meet their business requirements. This result demonstrates the role and unique niche of *The National Map* to meet the need for nationally consistent, seamless, and integrated geospatial data. Addressing this need is critically important to the long-term success of the USGS National Geospatial Program. The program should continue to embrace a partnership model to facilitate access to the most current and highest quality data. Survey results indicate that data-integration needs would be better achieved with participation from Federal, State, and local data stewards. Additionally, research and development activities should be focused on technologies that dramatically improve data-integration capabilities and customer access to these datasets.

2. The National Map *awareness and brand recognition.*—When asked, customers were unable to describe or list products and services of *The National Map*. Further, there was uncertainty as to how FGDC, Geospatial One-Stop (GOS), the National Atlas of the United States®, and other USGS services were related to *The National Map*. Customers expressed frustration over the vast array of services that were difficult to navigate through. In some instances, customers were finding broken links and services that are no longer relevant. It is difficult for many

customers to know the differences among a DLG (digital line graph), a DRG (digital raster graphic), a GeoPDF scanned topographic map, and a next-generation GeoPDF image map. Similar situations are found with the various online viewer services. The USGS geospatial product lines need to be clearly identified, and external communications, marketing, and branding of USGS National Geospatial Program services need to be improved. Recent improvements to *The National Map* Web site, the addition of the Product and Services Directory (Newell, 2008), and the ongoing development of the online viewer for *The National Map* are making significant advances toward meeting this need.

Customer Data Requirements for *The National Map*

3. *Geospatial framework data priority needs.*—The highest priority datasets are imagery, elevation, public streets and roads, surface water, civil boundaries, parcels, land cover, geographic names, Public Land Survey System, vertical and horizontal control, and Federal and Native American land boundaries. All of these datasets received a high rating by at least 30 percent of all customers surveyed. Limited funding for *The National Map* should be directed to these highest priority datasets. Detailed data requirements should be developed for each of these data types in accordance with the OMB A–16 supplemental lifecycle guidance (currently in draft, Office of Management and Budget, 2008). Data layers such as trails, springs and wells, and rural area structures that received a lower priority rating were rated highly for specialized applications. For example, structures in rural areas are very important to emergency responders. Many of these lower priority rating datasets also enhance *The National Map* published topographic map product. The USGS should rely on partner contributions through improved coordination and standards setting activities by the FGDC and as outlined in the OMB A–16 directive to meet these needs without spending National Geospatial Program funds on lower priority data layers.

4. *Geospatial data beyond framework layers.*—USGS customer interview and ASPRS survey participants were asked to rate the importance of geospatial data layers that are not currently included within *The National Map*. All 12 data layers were ranked as "somewhat important" or higher, indicating a high interest for additional national level data layers. Prompted by this question were many requests to expand the scope to include more than the eight geospatial base data layers managed under the umbrella of *The National Map* today. A procedure is needed to evaluate and make decisions about adding, dropping, or modifying content of data layers. Currently, existing layers evolve over time to incorporate new

geospatial components. For example, watershed boundaries are being added to the NHD, effectively adding a new feature to *The National Map*. There are implications for long-term data lifecycle costs, and *The National Map* program priorities need to be taken into consideration. While this action was endorsed by the NHD community and would likely be viewed as a good direction by all parties, a process for making this type of decision within the community for *The National Map* would receive broader customer and partner support.

5. *Geospatial data scale and resolution.*—The discussion of geospatial data scale and resolution was often influenced by concerns for computing capacity and network bandwidth needed to utilize very large datasets. Customers found it difficult to think about the business problems they were trying to address apart from these technical limitations that affected work productivity. Conversely, it is important that the USGS not build national datasets at a scale or resolution that is affordable if it does not meet the customer requirements. This is a significant consideration as the USGS plans for the future, knowing that technology will continue to improve and acquisition costs for high-resolution data may decline with improved technology. As the needs change and the data acquisition costs drop, organizations are trending to higher resolution and more accurate data to meet their needs. While this observation cannot be validated by our survey results, interview discussions and responses to the wishes for *The National Map* revealed this to be a significant trend. The geospatial data lifecycle plans need to address customer requirements for improved scale (accuracy) and resolution.

6. *Geospatial data quality.*—Positional accuracy was identified as the most important quality-control issue over attribute accuracy, completeness, and currency. Customers did not want to be put in a position of ranking one data quality component over another, indicating that they are all critically important. There was a perspective, however, that positional accuracy of features was a core component of a quality database and that a data steward (such as a State partner) could more effectively address improvements in the form of new features or correction of attributes. The overall positional accuracy of *The National Map* could be significantly improved if the imagery, elevation, and vertical and horizontal control (and possibly the land survey) data layers could be modernized with current high-resolution data. These "foundational" data layers would then serve as the Nation's base for integrating and improving the quality of other data layers. If these foundation data are to be the building block of future generations of *The National Map*, a data content specification needs to be developed, and an assessment should be completed to determine the capacity of partner organizations to contribute data to *The National Map* that will meet these requirements. Where gaps exist, plans should be developed to address the shortcomings.

7. *Geospatial data update requirements.*—The majority of regional or national level analysis and mapping needs could be satisfied with a 3-year update cycle. Exceptions include transportation and parcels, which need to be updated annually, and elevation data, which can be updated as infrequently as every 5 years. Those datasets that have a high rate of change, such as parcels and transportation, would require a very active stewardship and data-integration process. The associated costs of maintaining these programs must be taken into consideration when designing stewardship models and when completing lifecycle costs analysis. Data stewardship programs for national datasets should adhere to these requirements, and the topographic map product to be derived from the enterprise database should be republished on a 3-year cycle. This would be a dramatic improvement over the average 27-year age of a published topographic map today. Consideration should be given to a publish-on-demand model where any customer can create a topographic map from the latest enterprise database.

8. *Geospatial data historical retention.*—The results show that there is a wide distribution of need for historical geospatial data but that maintaining a few historical data layers could meet a majority of the need. Imagery and land cover were rated significantly higher than other data layers for their historical value. While land cover did not receive one of the highest ratings as a base geospatial data layer, it should be noted that over time, this data layer increases in value for certain applications. For this reason, the benefits analysis of a land cover mapping program should consider the value of these data for historical documentation as well as the intrinsic value for current land planning and management activities. Printed maps have acted as the archive media in the past. These existing print products should be scanned and maintained as a readily available digital archive. An evaluation of current archive procedures (for the purpose of historical retention as opposed to backup and recovery) should be completed.

9. *Data use restrictions.*—Most customers felt that *The National Map* data should be publicly available without license restrictions. If commercial datasets are used in *The National Map* products or services, the data should be publicly available under the terms of a public use agreement. The National Geospatial Program should assess the feasibility and associated costs of acquiring currently available commercial data through a competitive acquisition process that would result in a public use license which holds no restrictions on dataset use by either the USGS or customers who use data services of *The National Map*.

10. *Web services.*—Regardless of how the questions were asked or what specific service was being evaluated, customers almost always valued geospatial data access services more highly than Web viewing or map prod-

ucts. The National Geospatial Program should continue to acquire high-quality data through State and Federal partnerships and expand data integration and data quality assurance activities within the program. Because customers place a high value on nationally consistent and integrated data, the data-delivery services must be more responsive to customer needs. Specific product services such as Web viewing and topographic map publishing are also important to a large customer base. A focus on data will also result in lower production costs for these other valued services because they will not have to absorb or incur the costs of making data improvements within the respective service offerings.

Topographic Map Product Requirements

11. *Need for a topographic map.*—Nearly 60 percent of respondents in the structured interviews and in the ASPRS survey said that a topographic map was quite important or very important to meeting their mission needs. While GIS professionals everywhere expressed a high need for the data, it was the lack of readily available, current, and standardized published products that frustrated field managers, emergency responders, and others. Requirements for published content have changed, and customers expect to have improved capabilities to generate custom USGS map products.

12. *Topographic content, publishing schedule, and quality.*—Customers expressed a willingness to accept a tradeoff in content richness, production schedules, and cartographic quality represented on a topographic map. While customers understood that the enterprise databases had variable data quality, they were less likely to accept data quality tradeoffs in order to achieve feature-rich content or high production rates. Further evaluation of the production-ready topographic map product is recommended to validate the suitability of the new topographic map product for specific business applications. Customer focus group workshops would provide timely feedback to the topographic map production team. Because the production design incorporates an iterative improvement process, feedback can be taken into consideration immediately for the next production cycle.

Next Steps

The results of the research on customer requirements identified a set of high-priority data, services, and online viewing requirements to inform planning activities for future versions of *The National Map*. The findings above that focus on customer requirements and priorities for data layers (findings 3, 4, 6, and 8) provide some general design direction for *The National Map*. Specifically, there should be a goal to significantly improve positional accuracy consistent with the needs of our customers. This goal would require modernizing and improving geospatial content positional accuracy of at least imagery and elevation. The geodetic control data should be evaluated for its suitability to support this requirement. Further, imagery and elevation data were in the top four priorities across samples (finding 3), and imagery is the first priority across samples for historical needs (finding 4). These modernized and improved layers should form the foundation of *The National Map*. In turn, this foundation will enable the integration and improvement of other data layers.

All four of these data-centric findings (including finding 6 concerning data beyond framework layers), suggest that in addition to the foundation layers, the layers most important to customers are transportation, boundaries, hydrography, and parcels. In every question, these layers were within the top six priorities. Further, when asked about their wishes for *The National Map*, customers' wishes with regard to data also mirrored this same priority list: imagery, elevation/LiDAR, hydrography, transportation, parcels, and boundaries.

The findings begin an important public discussion to set program priorities for *The National Map*. Further, the findings strongly point to *The National Map* as a geospatial base data framework for the Nation. Consumers of these geospatial services will use nationally consistent base data with their own services to create products like disaster response maps, task orders, trail maps, mortgage foreclosure forecast maps, flood inundation maps, resource management plans, census field maps, and topographic maps. The participation of State, Federal, and private sector partners will be critical to the successful creation of unified services that span the levels of government and use that is envisioned.

The research team is grateful for the many hours spent by our customers sharing their aspirations for improvements to *The National Map*. The feedback that was received has already had a profound effect on our operational program. All of the base datasets are being improved, but limited funds are being focused on the highest priority datasets. The new topographic map product will focus on quality and higher production rates and less on full content. *The National Map* viewer is receiving a major overhaul and when released, it will have fewer data layers but will feature national coverage of seamless data layers and improved system performance. Maybe the most important findings were the needs to stay in touch with our customers, to improve our product messaging, and to assess the changing business requirements on an ongoing basis.

John Wesley Powell testified before Congress on December 5, 1884. He advocated for the creation of a United States map. In that testimony, he said "A Government cannot do any scientific work of more value to the people at large, than by causing the construction of proper topographic maps of the country." The digital age equivalent of the Powell mapping expedition is urgently needed!

References Cited

National Atlas of the United States®, 2009, National Atlas of the United States®: available only online at http://nationalatlas.gov. (Accessed September 28, 2009.) (The atlas includes maps and data layers from more than 20 Federal organizations.)

National Research Council, Committee on Land Parcel Databases, 2007, National land parcel data; A vision for the future: Washington, D.C., National Academies Press, 172 p., available online at http://www.nap.edu/catalog.php?record_id=11978#description.

Newell, M.R., 2008, *The National Map* product and services directory: U.S. Geological Survey Fact Sheet 2008–3065, 4 p., available online at http://pubs.usgs.gov/fs/2008/3065/.

Office of Management and Budget, 2002, Coordination of geographic information and related spatial data activities (revised edition): Office of Management and Budget Circular A–16, available at http://www.whitehouse.gov/omb/rewrite/Circulars/a016/a016_rev.html.

Office of Management and Budget, 2008, Geospatial line of business, OMB Circular A–16 supplemental guidance: 95 p. (Draft guidance of December 10, 2008, endorsed by the Federal Geographic Data Committee available at http://www.fgdc.gov/policyandplanning/A-16-supplemental-guidance-endorsed-dec08.pdf.)

U.S. Census Bureau, 2009, TIGER® [Topologically Integrated Geographic Encoding and Referencing system], TIGER/Line® and TIGER®-related products: available at http://www.census.gov/geo/www/tiger/.

U.S. Geological Survey, 2009, *The National Map*: U.S. Geological Survey database at http://nationalmap.gov/index.html. (Accessed August 31, 2009.)